What's Your Opera I.Q.?

What's Your OPERA I.Q.?

OVER 100 QUIZZES FOR OPERA LOVERS

Iris Bass

A Citadel Press Book
Published by Carol Publishing Group

Carol Publishing Group Edition, 1997

A Citadel Press Book
Published by Carol Publishing Group
Citadel Press is a registered trademark of Carol Communications, Inc.

Editorial, sales and distribution, rights and permissions inquiries should be addressed to Carol Publishing Group, 120 Enterprise Avenue, Secaucus, N.J. 07094

In Canada: Canadian Manda Group, One Atlantic Avenue, Suite 105, Toronto, Ontario M6K 3E7

Carol Publishing Group books may be purchased in bulk at special discounts for sales promotion, fund-raising, or educational purposes. Special editions can be created to specifications. For details, contact Special Sales Department, Carol Publishing Group, 120 Enterprise Avenue, Secaucus, N.J. 07094.

Manufactured in the United States of America
10 9 8 7 6 5 4 3 2 1

Library of Congress Cataloging-in-Publication Data

Bass, Iris.
    What's your opera I.Q.? : over 100 quizzes for opera lovers / Iris Bass.
        p.   cm.
    "A Citadel Press book."
    ISBN 0-8065-1862-6 (pbk.)
    1. Opera—Miscellanea.   I. Title.
ML1700.B17   1997
782.1—dc21   96-50272
                                                                CIP
                                                                MN

TO ONE OF THE ANSWERS.
TO ALL OF THEM.

Introduction to the Revised Edition

THERE EXISTS an entire generation of operagoers not raised on the old Met and Maria Callas—people to whom listening to even an LP has become as outmoded as playing an Edison cylinder recording. Yet opera is far from a dead art. Perhaps the finest proof of its vigor may lie in a comparison of the first edition of *What's Your Opera I.Q.?* (published in 1991) and this revised edition, reworked five years later. The original 100 quizzes have been updated and also expanded to now number 130; and the 500-odd operas, operettas, musical comedies, and opera-related films and plays covered in the former edition have grown to a whopping 700. These amazing figures are a reflection of greater accessibility of rarer works via live performance or CDs, as well as new layman-level interest in opera fostered by the "Three Tenors" concerts and such shows as *Miss Saigon*.

Written with a particular view toward what has been happening in the last twenty-five years, *What Your Opera I.Q.?* encompasses a broad repertoire that ranges from Monteverdi to Glass. Sources include such current reference books as the 1993 *Who's Who in British Opera* as well as historic works like Kobbé's original 1919 *The Complete Opera Book*; libretti of hundreds of works being performed and recorded by contemporary artists; over fifteen years of worldwide journalistic coverage in *Opera News* and *Opera*; and the author's own attendance at live performances dating back to her first in-theater opera in 1971.

This revised edition of *What's Your Opera I.Q.?* brings readers up to date on black opera history, and works featuring Native American, Central and South American, and Asian artists or subject matter; telecasts, films, recordings, and books; and U.S. regional companies and summer festivals. While the book does contain items about the past, it also looks forward to things to come, documenting works that had their world premiere virtually within weeks of the new manuscript's completion date.

Instructional as well as fun, and better than ever, *What's Your Opera I.Q.?* is a detailed, scrupulously researched, yet light-hearted—even irreverant—celebration of the vitality and madness of opera.

Author's Note

(An Apology to Tchaikovsky *et al.*)

MANY OF THESE QUIZZES were created by working with standard editions of opera libretti—that is, from the original language portion of them. As operagoers are ever-distressed to learn, when texts are translated into English, whether for performance purposes or simple understanding, data such as numbers and object names may be changed in order to fit rhyme or meter. Also, idiomatic foreign expressions may be adjusted drastically to make sense in idiomatic English. Furthermore, English translations vary from edition to edition: one may have to make do with archaic poetic nonsense or may just as easily come upon a libretto that has been tailored to suit a specific modern staging. What's a quiz writer to do? For the sake of consistency and accuracy, I have gone to the original language of French, German, Italian, and Spanish operatic works when writing quizzes based upon their texts.

Because I cannot read Czech, Russian, or other Eastern languages, and cannot quite trust English translations of them for the above reasons, such operas do not appear in quizzes that require a fine knowledge of the wording of such libretti. Meanwhile, I have taken care to include many modern American and British works that I feel have gotten short shrift in other quiz books.

In choosing what works will be included overall, I have gone by the following definition: an opera is a vocal musical and dramatic work performed in an opera house. Thus, this book encompasses not only opera but also operetta and crossover musical comedies. A list of all works mentioned in the book appears as an appendix.

I hope that these quizzes will inspire their readers to explore the intricacies of this fascinating art form for themselves, in all its visual and aural glory. After the bits and pieces have provided you with hours of enjoyable mental gymnastics, do pursue the entire original sources for even greater pleasure!

Questions

1. BLUE BLOOD

Can you name the composers of the following operatic works?

1. *Le Roi d'Ys*
2. *L'Amore dei Tre Re*
3. *The King Goes Forth to France*
4. *Anna Bolena*
5. *Le Roi Malgré Lui*
6. *Elisabetta, Regina d'Inghilterra*
7. *A Life for the Tsar*
8. *Mary, Queen of Scots*
9. *Le Roi L'A Dit*
10. *Ivan IV*
11. *The Tsar's Bride*
12. *Königskinder*
13. *Le Roi de Lahore*
14. *Henry VIII*
15. *La Reine de Saba*

Extra Credit:

A. Of what country does Eurydice's guard claim he was once king, in *Orphée aux Enfers?*

B. Beverly Sills performed the roles of seven queens with New York City Opera. What were they?

C. What is the name of Verdi's only comic opera aside from *Falstaff?*

2. DOUBLE ENTENDRES

While representing, in all cases, totally different characters, the character names listed at left each crop up in *two* operas listed at right (some popular names appear in even more works not listed here as choices). Can you match each name to two operas?

1. Elvira	a.	*Mefistofele*
2. Leonora	b.	*Luisa Miller*
3. Arturo	c.	*Lucia di Lammermoor*
4. Lindoro	d.	*Werther*
5. Amelia	e.	*Il Barbiere di Siviglia*
6. Susanna	f.	*La Forza del Destino*
7. Marcellina	g.	*L'Italiana in Algeri*
8. Paolo	h.	*Un Ballo in Maschera*
9. Ferrando	i.	*Francesca da Rimini*
10. Marie	j.	*La Fille du Régiment*
11. Tonio	k.	*I Puritani*
12. Sophie	l.	*Khovanshchina*
13. Rodolfo	m.	*Così Fan Tutte*
14. Andrei	n.	*Wozzeck*
15. Enrico	o.	*Simon Boccanegra*
	p.	*Pagliacci*
	q.	*Fidelio*
	r.	*Der Rosenkavalier*
	s.	*Le Nozze di Figaro*
	t.	*La Bohème*
	u.	*Il Trovatore*
	v.	*War and Peace*

Extra Credit:

Match each composer at left to his opera at right.

A. Richard Strauss	i.	*Drei Wältzer*
B. Johann Strauss II	ii.	*Padmâvatî*
C. Oscar Straus	iii.	*Les Indes Galantes*

D. Jean-Jacques Rousseau
E. Albert Roussel
F. Jean-Philippe Rameau

iv. *Die Schweigsame Frau*
v. *Le Devin du Village*
vi. *Der Zigeunerbaron*

3. TRIPLETS

Match each name at left to the opera in which the character appears at right.

1. Adina
2. Amina
3. Annina
4. Paquillo
5. Pedrillo
6. Pinellino
7. Fiorilla
8. Fiora
9. Fiordiligi
10. Belfiore
11. Belcore
12. Belmonte
13. Ottavio
14. Octavian
15. Ottavia

a. *Gianni Schicchi*
b. *Il Turco in Italia*
c. *L'Amore dei Tre Re*
d. *La Sonnambula*
e. *L'Elisir d'Amore*
f. *Der Rosenkavalier*
g. *L'Incoronazione di Poppea*
h. *La Finta Giardiniera*
i. *Die Entführung aus dem Serail*
j. *La Périchole*
k. *Don Giovanni*
l. *La Traviata*
m. *Così Fan Tutte*

Extra Credit:

And to make each a quartet, match the following characters to their operas:

A. Aminta
B. Pizarro
C. Florinda
D. Belinda
E. Ottone

i. *Fidelio*
ii. *Dido and Aeneas*
iii. *Die Schweigsame Frau*
iv. *L'Incoronazione di Poppea*
v. *Le Donne Curiose*

4. OOPS!

The answer to this quiz is simple, if you know your opera history. What do the following works have in common?

1. *La Traviata*
2. Rossini's *Il Barbiere di Siviglia*
3. *Carmen*
4. *Edgar*
5. *Tristan und Isolde*
6. *Julien*
7. *A Midsummer Marriage*
8. *Mefistofele*
9. *Guntram*
10. *Beatrice di Tenda*

Extra Credit:

What opera, which premiered at the Met in 1942, is unperformable today as a complete work, and why?

5. SIBLING RIVALRY

Can you match the operatic characters at left to their brothers and sisters at right?

1. Gualtiero	a. Zdenka
2. Lucia	b. Alberich
3. Fiordiligi	c. Tisbe
4. Charlotte	d. Rochefort
5. Cunegonde	e. Tolomeo
6. Sieglinde	f. Giorgio
7. Feodor	g. Dorabella
8. Arabella	h. Enrico
9. Mime	i. Xenia
10. Cleopatra	j. Dorothée
11. Clorinda	k. Sparafucile
12. Noémie	l. Siegmund
13. Anna Bolena	m. Sophie
14. Maddalena	n. Maximilian

Extra Credit:

A. What is the relationship of Steva and Laca in *Jenůfa* (or, similarly, Jenik and Vašek in *The Bartered Bride*)?

B. In *Robert le Diable*, how are Alice and the title character related?

C. *Libuše* concerns three siblings. What are their names?

6. OTHER VOICES, OTHER ROOMS

The lines at left are traditionally performed offstage. Can you match them to their operas? For extra credit, identify their situations.

1. *"A una fonta afflitto…"*
2. "Momus, Momus, Momus, *Zitti e discreti andiamoscene via"*
3. *"Magnificat anima mea Dominum"*
4. *"Vi sfido"*
5. *"Zurück!"*
6. *"O Lola, ch'ai di latti la cammisa"*
7. *"Largo al quadrupede sir della festa"*
8. *"Gittate i palischermi"*
9. *"Ave Signor degli angelle del santi"*
10. *"Sauvée!"*
11. *"Jesu vient de naître…"*
12. *"De mon amie, fleur endormie"*
13. *"Blanche Dourga…"*
14. *"Circe, Circe, kannst du mich hören?"*
15. *"Glou! glou! glou!"*

a. *Tosca*
b. *La Traviata*
c. *Les Contes d'Hoffmann*
d. *Werther*
e. *La Bohème*
f. *Cavalleria Rusticana*
g. *Ariadne auf Naxos*
h. *Manon*
i. *Faust*
j. *Les Pêcheurs de Perles*
k. *I Puritani*
l. *Otello*
m. *Lakmé*
n. *Mefistofele*
o. *Die Zauberflöte*

7. NOMS DE TUNE

These famous singers began their lives with the following names. Can you guess their stage names?

1. Rose Ponzillo
2. Maria Kalogeropoulos
3. Jacob Perelmuth
4. Rose Calvet
5. Helen Mitchell
6. Reba Fiersohn
7. Louise Beatty
8. George Burnstein
9. Ernst Seiffert
10. Ernestine Rössler
11. Jan Mieczisław
12. Praxede Kochańska
13. Morris Miller
14. Alfredo Trujillo
15. Gerard Tisserand

Extra Credit:

A. Which director's name is really Gian Franco Corsi?

B. Which librettist began life as Emmanuele Conegliano?

C. What was Titta Ruffo's real name?

8. THE POWER OF THE PEN

Below, a list of popular operas. What do they have in common regarding their libretti?

1. *Intermezzo*
2. *Trouble in Tahiti*
3. *Mefistofele*
4. *Louise*
5. *Wozzeck*
6. *Carmina Burana*
7. *Les Troyens*
8. *Jenůfa*
9. *Tristan und Isolde*
10. *The Medium*
11. *Pagliacci*
12. *Rusalka*
13. *A Midsummer Marriage*
14. *The Gambler*
15. *Susannah*

Extra Credit:

A. What famous novelist wrote the libretto of *L'Enfant et les Sortilèges?*

B. What famous stage and film director created the libretto of Barber's *Antony and Cleopatra?*

C. What famous tenor co-authored the libretto of *A Midsummer Night's Dream?*

9. THE CHILDREN'S ARIA

"Children should be seen and not heard" goes the familiar saying. While some of the following are indeed mute parts, the pint-sized characters described here all have names. What are they?

1. The little blackamoor in *Der Rosenkavalier.*
2. The Tabor child "renamed" by William Jennings Bryan in *The Ballad of Baby Doe.*
3. Emile de Becque's son in *South Pacific.*
4. Boris Godunov's young son in *Boris Godunov.*
5. Guillaume Tell's young son in *Guillaume Tell.*
6. Juana's little girl in *La Loca.*
7. Gherardo and Nella's child in *Gianni Schicchi.*
8. The little boy in *Albert Herring.*
9. The young hero of *Where the Wild Things Are.*
10. Rose's kid brother in *Street Scene.*

Extra Credit:

What are the names of the Le Bailli's eight children in *Werther?*

10. MOONLIGHTING

The composers at left are now more famous for their instrumental works or conducting, but each man also wrote at least one opera—in fact, Vivaldi penned over forty, and Scarlatti some 115! Can you match each work at right to its composer?

1. Liszt	a.	*Genoveva*
2. Ravel	b.	*L'Enfant et les Sortilèges*
3. Schubert	c.	*At the Boar's Head*
4. Scarlatti	d.	*Pousse d'Amour*
5. Fauré	e.	*The Tender Land*
6. Walton	f.	*Hin und Zurück*
7. Vivaldi	g.	*Don Sanche*
8. Holst	h.	*Fierrabras*
9. Copland	i.	*The Nose*
10. Schumann	j.	*Aleko*
11. Satie	k.	*Pénélope*
12. Hermann	l.	*Montezuma*
13. Shostakovich	m.	*Troilus and Cressida*
14. Rachmaninov	n.	*Wuthering Heights*
15. Hindemith	o.	*Mitridate Eupatore*

Extra Credit:

A. Four of "The Five" Russian composers wrote operas. Match each man to his respective work.

I. Borodin	i.	*The Saracen*
II. Mussorgsky	ii.	*Sadko*
III. Cui	iii.	*Prince Igor*
IV. Rimsky-Korsakov	iv.	*Khovanshchina*

B. Four of "Les Six" French composers also wrote operas. Match them.

V. Auric	v.	*Jeanne d'Arc au Bûcher*
VI. Honegger	vi.	*Les Malheurs d'Orphée*
VII. Milhaud	vii.	*La Voix Humaine*
VIII. Poulenc	viii.	*Sous le Masque*

11. THE MAN BEHIND THE MYTH

The original ideas for some operatic plots trace all the way back to Ancient Greece. Can you name the people whose epic dramas, stories, and poems form the basis of the following works? (Example: the man behind *Dido and Aeneas* was Virgil.)

1. *Elektra*
2. *Alceste*
3. *L'Incoronazione di Poppea*
4. *King Priam*
5. *Les Troyens*
6. *Iphigénie en Tauride*
7. *Daphne*
8. *Médée*
9. *Philémon et Baucis*
10. *Oedipus Rex*

Extra Credit:

A. Metamorphoses occur in several operas. What do the following characters change into?

  i. Jupiter *Die Liebe der Danae*
  ii. Jupiter *Orphée aux Enfers*
  iii. Daphne *Daphne*
  iv. Acis *Acis and Galatea*

B. *The Rape of Lucretia* has roots that go back not only to Shakespeare, but beyond him to Ancient Rome. What Roman writer supplied the earliest inspirations?

C. Stephen Sondheim wrote music for a Greek drama "staged" in 1974 in the Yale swimming pool. What was it, and who was the original playwright?

12. SPARE PARTS

The following arias or ensembles start with a reference to specific areas of the human anatomy. Can you identify the operas they come from?

1. "Come to my Arms, my lovely Fair"
2. "Our arms intertwined"
3. *"O dolci mani"* (hands)
4. *"Al tuoi piedi ci prostriamo"* (feet)
5. "Silvered is the raven hair"
6. *"En fermant les yeux"* (eyes)
7. "To pull-a da toot" (tooth)
8. *"In mia man alfin tu sei"* (hand)
9. *"Sa main, sa douce main"* (hand)
10. *"Il me semble sur mon épaule"* (shoulder)
11. "Take a pair of sparkling eyes"
12. *"Sanft schloss Schlaf dein Aug"* (eyes)
13. *"Placa l'alma, quieta il petto"* (chest)
14. *"O grandi occhi"* (eyes)
15. *"Ferme tes yeux"* (eyes)

Extra Credit:

What are the fourteen areas of the body named in "A British tar is a soaring soul" from *H.M.S. Pinafore?*

13. CALL ME...IRRESPONSIBLE

Opera has given birth to some of the oddest names outside the novels of Dickens. Can you identify the works in which these characters appear?

1. Johnny Inkslinger
2. Lady Billows
3. Fireball Snedeker
4. Ko-Ko-Ri-Ko
5. Peep-Bo
6. Carl Worms
7. Dr. Turtlespit
8. Little Bat
9. Snout
10. Mr. Splinters
11. Muff
12. Schlemiel

13. Peccadillo   15. Pantaloon
14. General Boum

Extra Credit:

In some operas, characters have descriptive titles rather than actual names. What operas do these groups of people appear in?

A. The Secretary, the Foreign Woman, the Secret-Police Agent

B. Hunchback, One-Eye, One-Arm

C. The Music Master, the Composer, the Wig Master, the Dancing Master

D. The Princess, the Abbess, the Monitor

E. The Captain, the Drum Major, the Doctor

F. A Man With Old Luggage, A Lady With a Cake Box, A Man With a Paint Box

14. FOOTNOTES

How well have you been watching singers' feet—or the conductor's beat?

1. What character must dance a hornpipe in *Ruddigore?*

2. In what act of *Eugene Onegin* is a polonaise danced?

3. In what act of the same work is a waltz danced?

4. In what act of *Boris Godunov* does a polonaise occur?

5. In *Manon*, what kind of dance is played as an entr'acte before Act III?

6. What Johann Strauss operetta contains the "*Schatz*" waltz?

7. What is the first dance to be named in Act I, Scene 2, of *War and Peace?*

8. What dance does Dolohov announce?

9. What Gilbert and Sullivan character says he can perform a "saraband, gondolet, carole, Pimpernel, or Jumping Joan"?

10. In *Orphée aux Enfers,* the famous Act IV cancan is called what kind of dance by its performers?

11. What kind of dance immediately precedes its first appearance in that act?

12. What kind of dance concludes Act I of *The Bartered Bride?*

13. What 3/4-time Bohemian dance is used as an orchestral interlude in Act II of that opera?

14. What kind of dance is done at the party in Act I of *Andrea Chénier?*

15. In Scene 22 of *Don Giovanni,* what do Don Ottavio and Donna Anna dance together?

Extra Credit:

A. In Act IV of *La Bohème,* the young roommates amuse themselves by dancing. What five dances do they announce?

B. What four dances are specified to take place in Act III of *Peter Grimes?*

C. In *Gloriana,* what three period dances are colorfully performed in Act II, Scene 3?

15. TWENTIETH-CENTURY TEAMWORK

Operas are usually referred to as works by such-and-such composer. Can you match the twentieth-century works at left to their librettists?

1. *Of Mice and Men*	a. Horace Everett
2. *Peter Grimes*	b. Maurice Lena
3. *The Crucible*	c. T. Ricordi
4. *The Tender Land*	d. Jack Larson
5. *Maria Golovin*	e. Giovacchino Forzano
6. *Dialogues des Carmélites*	f. Montague Slater
7. *Lord Byron*	g. Gian Carlo Menotti
8. *Francesca da Rimini*	h. Gertrude Stein

9. *L'Amore dei Tre Re*
10. *Le Jongleur de Notre-Dame*
11. *Il Tabarro*
12. *Die Tote Stadt*
13. *Lodoletta*
14. *King Priam*
15. *The Mother of Us All*

i. Sen Benelli
j. Carlisle Floyd
k. Michael Tippett
l. Bernard Stambler
m. Paul Schott
n. Giuseppe Adami
o. Georges Bernanos

Extra Credit:

A. Novelist E. M. Forster was partly responsible for a libretto of a well-known Britten opera. What was it?

B. What famous composer had a hand in the libretto for Henze's *Elegy for Young Lovers?*

C. What composer is the librettist for Barber's *Vanessa?*

16. THE PERFECT WAGNERITE

Those of you who enjoy Wagner are blessed with the stamina to sit through *Die Meistersinger* (nearly six hours, counting intermissions) or a four-evening *Ring.* But how well did you pay attention during such events?

1. A total of how many tones and melodies does David's aria list as having to be mastered by a singer?

2. A minimum of how many faults will disqualify a singer from the competition?

3. In *Die Meistersinger*, who are, collectively, Christian, Peter, Niklaus, and Hans?

4. Which *Ring* character sings the line *"Wagalaweia! Wallala weiala weia"?*

5. Which *Ring* character sings the line *"Hehe! Hehe! Hieher! Hieher!"?*

6. Which Wagnerian character sings *"Heiha! Hei ha ha ha ha!"?*

7. Which of Wagner's operas includes the refrain *"Hohohe! Jolohe! Hoho! Ho! Ho!"*?

8. What is the name of the sword that Siegmund pulls from the ashtree?

9. About which goddess does the Shepherd in *Tannhäuser* sing?

10. Who sneezes while climbing about the rocks of the Rhine?

11. What mortal woman bears Alberich's child?

12. In a bit of Valkyrie humor, why should Ortlinde's and Helmwige's horses not be stabled together?

13. Who speaks the name of the yet unborn Parsifal just before dying?

14. Which of Wagner's operas was not performed until five years after his death?

15. What is Siegfried's "Achilles' heel"?

Extra Credit:

Match the Meistersingers to their trades.

A.	Hans Sachs	a.	baker
B.	Veit Pogner	b.	town clerk
C.	Kunz Vogelgesang	c.	coppersmith
D.	Konrad Nachtigall	d.	goldsmith
E.	Sixtus Beckmesser	e.	soapboiler
F.	Fritz Kothner	f.	stocking maker
G.	Balthasar Zorn	g.	tinsmith
H.	Ulrich Eisslinger	h.	shoemaker
I.	Augustin Moser	i.	furrier
J.	Hermann Ortel	j.	pewterer
K.	Hans Schwartz	k.	tailor
L	Hans Foltz	l.	grocer

17. STORMY WEATHER

Neither snow nor rain...makes the curtain go down on the following scenes. Can you identify the operas in which these take place?

1. What composer wrote a children's opera called *The Second Hurricane?*

2. Although she knocks at the door seeking shelter from the rain, the soprano knows that her entry means certain death.

3. A storm drives a hunter and huntress into each other's arms.

4. A doomed sailor is driven by storm into a Norwegian harbor.

5. Thunder rages as two enemies plan to settle a family feud with a duel.

6. An incestuous relationship gets its start during a rainstorm.

7. A tempest rocks the hero's boat as he sails home in triumph from battle.

8. Villagers become still more distrustful of the leading man when he sings a strange song during a squall.

9. A prince and his servant dry off at a peasant girl's house a few days after a ball which even she has attended.

10. A raging blizzard does not prevent a posse from pursuing their prey.

Extra Credit:

A. In what light opera, by a French composer better known for a serious grand opera, does a major character lose his sight during a storm?

B. In what opera by a famous German composer do two characters first meet on a ski slope?

C. In what Italian verismo opera does the heroine die in the snow outside her lover's house?

18. LAST WORKS

If you've had it up to here with all those child prodigies who penned full-length operas in their cribs, let's see how good you are at naming the LAST words (as determined by the operas' premiere dates) by the following composers. Brownie points if you can also remember who didn't live to finish the job themselves.

1. Verdi
2. Puccini
3. Bizet
4. Offenbach
5. Prokofiev
6. Rossini
7. Sullivan
8. Bellini
9. Wagner
10. Meyerbeer
11. Britten
12. Mozart
13. Tchaikovsky
14. R. Strauss
15. Rimsky-Korsakov

Extra Credit:

Donizetti produced three operas in his final year of opera composition. What were they, and which was the very last to premiere?

19. CROSSOVERS

Musicals have been wending their way into the classical world. Can you name the composer/lyricist teams responsible for the following works?

1. *Carousel*
2. *West Side Story*
3. *Porgy and Bess*
4. *Cinderella*
5. *My Fair Lady*
6. *Kiss Me Kate*
7. *The Most Happy Fella*
8. *South Pacific*
9. *Candide*
10. *Kismet*
11. *Brigadoon*
12. *Song of Norway*
13. *The Pajama Game*
14. *The Sound of Music*
15. *A Little Night Music*

Extra Credit:

A. Who donated five million dollars—a million per year—to New York City Opera in exchange for the company's mounting of its 1986-1990 musical comedy spring season?

B. Who is the lyricist of George Gershwin's one-act jazz opera, *Blue Monday*, composed for the revue entitled *Scandals of 1922?*

C. What member of the famed Algonquin Round Table contributed lyrics to the original *Candide?*

20. OK, WHO STARTED IT?

A dramatic device frequently used in opera is an ensemble in which all action stops as the principal characters tell the audience their feelings and thoughts (which they are still keeping private from each other). For each of the following, can you identify the character who begins the ensemble?

1. *Rigoletto* Act III Quartet
2. *Lucia di Lammermoor* Act II Sextet
3. *Les Contes d'Hoffmann* Venice Sextet
4. *Manon* Finale of Act IV
5. *Maria Stuarda* Act II concluding Sextet
6. *Faust* concluding Trio
7. *Il Barbiere di Siviglia* Final Trio
8. *La Traviata* Finale of Act II, Scene 2
9. *Die Zauberflöte* Finale
10. *Roméo et Juliette,* Finale Act III, Scene 2

Extra Credit:

Name the four singers of the *"Puritani* Quartet" and their roles.

21. WORLD OPERA

How well-traveled are you, musically speaking?

1. What was the first opera presented at the Opéra Bastille when it opened in March 1990?

2. What Brazilian theater reopened for opera performance in 1990 after a hiatus of ninety-two years?

3. The Kirov Opera of St. Petersburg *and* the St. Petersburg National Opera each made their American debut in what year?

4. In early 1991, curtain time of what Israeli Opera production was delayed ten days by the Gulf Crisis?

5. In what city is there an annual Berlioz Festival?

6. In what country does the Ravenna Festival take place?

7. In what country does the Ravinia Festival take place?

8. *Satyagraha* was commissioned by the Arts Council of what city?

9. What opera, postponed for two years so that the tenor for whom the title role was written could star in it, finally had its world premiere in Barcelona in 1989?

10. What was the first Western operatic work ever to be sung in the Cairo Opera House in Arabic, in 1961?

11. What Italian city hosts an annual Rossini Festival?

12. Torre del Lago hosts an annual festival in honor of what twentieth-century composer?

13. In 1988, Richard Bonynge discovered "lost" manuscript pages to what opera while going through ballet scores in the basement of the Royal Opera House at Covent Garden?

14. What was the first foreign company to perform in the Metropolitan Opera House when it moved into its new home at Lincoln Center?

15. What opera was performed at Finland's Savonlinna Festival by the Central Opera of Peking in their first trip to the West in 1988—in Chinese?

Extra credit:

A. When the Vienna Volksoper made their U.S. debut in 1984, what three productions did they present?

B. What five operas did the Bolshoi Opera bring to the U.S. on their first tour to this country in 1975?

C. What four operas did the Teatro alla Scala bring to the U.S. in their first-ever tour to America in 1976?

22. FIRST THINGS FIRST

Into an article in *The Wall Street Journal* a writer let slip the misnomer *Antonio* Rossini. Can you do better with the given names of these composers?

1. Leoncavallo
2. Ponchielli
3. Auber
4. Smetana
5. Zandonai
6. Giordano
7. Bellini
8. Glinka
9. Donizetti
10. Kálmán

Extra Credit:

A. What was Giacomo Meyerbeer's entire real name?

B. What was Fromental Halévy's entire real name?

C. What *was* Rossini's first name?

23. ECHOES

Some operas quote from other musical works. How adept are you at *déjà-entendu?*

1. In *The Ballad of Baby Doe,* whom does the cast in Act I Scene I go to listen to (though we never do get to hear her)?

2. In *Don Giovanni,* Mozart quotes from one of his own operas. What aria is it?

3. What is the original name of the Irish air heard in *Martha?*

4. What is used for Pinkerton's "American" leitmotif?

5. What opera is heard in rehearsal during *Captain Jinks of the Horse Marines?*

6. In *Le Donne Curiose,* Wolf-Ferrari quotes from a Venetian barcarole. What is its title?

7. *Orphée aux Enfers* quotes a line from what Gluck opera?

8. In *Les Contes d'Hoffmann,* what Mozart aria does Nicklausse mockingly sing a little of?

9. What Gilbert and Sullivan operetta is named in *The Pirates of Penzance?*

10. What Schumann song does Dr. P sing in *The Man Who Mistook His Wife for a Hat?*

Extra Credit:

A. In *Don Giovanni,* onstage musicians play music from operas by two composers other than Mozart. Whose, and what are the operas?

B. What genuine school song is sung during *Street Scene?*

C. In what Offenbach operetta do young lovers who wish to marry plead their case with the girl's father in a pastiche bel canto trio sung in Italian doubletalk?

24. AN OPERA BY ANY OTHER NAME

Many subtitles of well-known works have disappeared into obscurity—perhaps with just cause! Below, translated into English, are some examples of these. Can you name their "supertitles"?

1. Wedded Love
2. The Vain Precaution

3. The Market of Richmond
4. The Witch's Curse
5. The Triumph of Goodness
6. The Count of Essex
7. The Lass That Loved a Sailor
8. The King of Bataria
9. The Slave of Duty
10. The Two Peters

Extra Credit:

A. What opera is subtitled "The Two Windows"?

B. What opera is subtitled "The Inn of Terracine"?

C. *Les Troyens* is really a double-bill of two works. Name them.

25. FIRST SIGHTINGS

Can you name the city in which each of the following operas had its world premiere?

1. *I Masnadieri*
2. *Werther*
3. *The Rake's Progress*
4. *Les Vêpres Siciliennes*
5. *Suor Angelica*
6. *The Turn of the Screw*
7. *Lulu*
8. *Don Pasquale*
9. *Così Fan Tutte*
10. *La Forza del Destino*
11. *La Clemenza di Tito*
12. *L'Enfant et les Sortilèges*
13. *Dialogues des Carmélites*
14. *The Gambler*
15. *I Puritani*

Extra Credit:

A. With what Verdi work did the Cairo Opera House open?

B. Where did the world premiere of *Amahl and the Night Visitors* take place?

C. Where did the first public opera house in the world open in 1637?

26. U.S. FESTIVALS

A valuable part of the American opera scene is its many music festivals, most of which take place during the summer.

1. What New York State summer arts community founded its own opera company in 1929?

2. Where did the PepsiCo Summerfare take place?

3. What avant-garde director enjoyed a close association with that festival?

4. *A Night at the Chinese Opera* had its U.S. premiere in what opera company's summer season?

5. At what U.S. festival did the American premiere of Wagner's *Das Liebesverbot* take place in 1983?

6. Which U.S. festival has presented, as of 1996, a total of eight world premieres and thirty-one American premieres, in addition to standard repertory?

7. At what New York City summer festival have such works as *La Finta Giardiniera, Idomeneo,* and *Acis and Galatea* been performed in concert form?

8. What U.S. music festival launched an all-American-cast *Ring* Cycle in 1985, believed to be the first of its kind?

9. In what city is Spoleto Festival USA based?

10. What opera has a special link with Central City Opera's summer season?

11. Why is *The Mighty Casey* a fitting feature of Glimmerglass Opera's repertoire?

12. In what U.S. state does Wolf Trap Opera perform?

13. In 1993, Santa Fe Opera produced the first American staging of Weill's first opera. What was it?

14. What opera company is based near New York's Glens Falls?

15. What opera company besides the Met has an annual summer season in New York City's Central Park?

Extra Credit:

A. Name the four Handel operas presented at Carnegie Hall's 1984-1985 Handel Festival in honor of the composer's 300th birthday year.

B. Name the four works in the opera-in-concert series presented by Carnegie Hall for its Centennial season, 1990-1991.

C. PepsiCo Summerfare concluded its existence in summer 1989 with three Mozart operas that had been performed there in past years—with much of the same casts. Name the operas that formed the 1989 program.

27. DOCTOR IN THE HOUSE

Can you match the doctors at left to the operas in which they appear? Note: Some are not necessarily doctors of *medicine*.

1. Dr. Malatesta	a. *Il Barbiere di Siviglia*
2. Don Prudenzio	b. *Die Fledermaus*
3. Dr. Buchanan	c. *L'Elisir d'Amore*
4. Dr. Faustus	d. *Help, Help, the*
5. Dr. Specialist	*Globolinks!*
6. Dr. Bartolo	e. *The Fiery Angel*
7. Dr. Caius	f. *Gianni Schicchi*
8. Dr. Blind	g. *Don Pasquale*
9. Dr. Dulcamara	h. *Osud*
10. Dr. Grenville	i. *Les Contes d'Hoffmann*
11. Dr. Stone	j. *The Cradle Will Rock*
12. Dr. Wilson	k. *La Traviata*
13. Maestro Spinellachio	l. *Falstaff*
14. Dr. Suda	m. *Il Viaggio a Reims*
15. Dr. Miracle	n. *Summer and Smoke*
	o. *Street Scene*

Extra Credit:

A. In *L'Amore Medico,* a suitor disguises himself as a doctor to gain access to his lover's home. Who is this opera's composer?

B. In 1857, Jacques Offenbach sponsored a competition for composers to create a score for a libretto entitled *Le Docteur Miracle*. Who won?

C. What real-life doctor was the inspiration for Despina's "cure" for the Albanians?

28. MISS-MATCHES

And, on the subject of personal titles, can you match these proper folk, at left, to the composers who wrote operas or operettas with those titles?

1. *Il Signor Bruschino*	a.	Offenbach
2. *Madame Pompadour*	b.	Giordano
3. *La Fille de Madame Angot*	c.	Cui
	d.	Rorem
4. *Miss Havisham's Fire*	e.	Messager
5. *Monsieur Choufleuri*	f.	Lecocq
6. *Mam-zelle Nitouche*	g.	Rossini
7. *Miss Julie*	h.	Argento
8. *Madame Sans-Gêne*	i.	Hervé
9. *Mam-zelle Fifi*	j.	Fall
10. *Madame Chrysanthème*	k.	Janáček
11. *Mlle. Modiste*	l.	Herbert
12. *Madame l'Archiduc*		
13. *Madame Favart*		
14. *Monsieur Beaucaire*		
15. *The Excursions of Mr. Brouček*		

Extra Credit:

A. What name is the equivalent of Cio-Cio-San in *M. Butterfly?*

B. What name is the equivalent of Cio-Cio-San in *Miss Saigon?*

C. Immediately following the wedding ceremony, Cio-Cio-San proclaims her new name. What is it?

29. TELECASTS

Lest we forget, opera only became a regular part of television programming in the 1970s.

1. Who sang the role of Madame Lidoine in the 1987 "Live from the Met" telecast of *Dialogues des Carmélites?*

2. Who portrayed Pinkerton in New York City Opera's 1982 simulcast of *Madama Butterfly?*

3. Who directed the Met's 1978 telecast of *Tosca,* in his first season as staging director with that company?

4. What Monty Python player performed the role of Ko-Ko in the English National Opera production of *The Mikado* broadcast in North America in 1988?

5. What British-born tenor sang the role of Nanki-Poo?

6. Who sang the title role in the Opera Company of Philadelphia's televised *Faust?*

7. What 1977 New York City Opera simulcast placed television audiences in the dilemma of having to choose between watching the opera or the World Series?

8. Audio-recording sessions of what album featuring Tatiana Troyanos, Kiri Te Kanawa, and José Carreras were telecast in 1985?

9. What opera filmed for television in 1992, trotted its cast about Rome to sing at the genuine sites and times of the day noted in the libretto?

10. Midway through their run of *Don Giovanni* during the Met's 1989-1990 season, basses Samuel Ramey and Ferruccio Furlanetto switched roles as the Don and Leporello. In the Salzburg production shown on U.S. television in 1988, which bass took which role?

11. Different telecasts in different years paired Beverly Sills and Plácido Domingo in special programs of music-related skits alongside a well-known actress-comedienne. Name her.

12. In 1984, PBS began showing a series of twelve Gilbert and Sullivan operettas cast with a combination of singers and actors. Who played Sir Despard Murgatroyd?

13. What tenor appeared as Don Ramiro in both the Ponnelle and Salzburg televised productions of *La Cenerentola?*

14. Who played the role when New York City Opera simulcast the work in the "Live from Lincoln Center" series?

15. In what year did the first televised "Pavarotti Plus!" concert take place?

Extra Credit:

A. Four artists in leading roles in the first "Live from the Met" telecast in 1977 appeared in another Met telecast of the same opera in 1982. Name the opera, the singers, and the roles they played.

B. The sets from five operas were used during the Met's two-part televised Centennial gala. Name the works the sets belonged to.

C. What five singers portrayed nineteenth-century concert artists in the 1985 "Rossini in Versailles" broadcast?

30. MASTER CLASSES

Opera is in a continuous state of evolution, as older composers teach their craft to younger ones. Can you match each composer at left to a composer at right who provided such direct instruction? Some of the answers may surprise you!

1. Adam	a. Schoenberg
2. Beeson	b. Boieldieu
3. Bizet	c. Milhaud
4. Berg	d. Zemlinsky
5. Charpentier	e. Rimsky-Korsakov
6. Blitzstein	f. Boito
7. Korngold	g. Cherubini

8. Gounod
9. Stravinsky
10. Vaughan Williams
11. Wolf-Ferrari
12. Glass
13. Boieldieu
14. Ravel
15. Delibes

h. Bartók
i. Fauré
j. Gounod
k. Adam
l. Massenet
m. Halévy
n. Ravel

Extra Credit:

A. Which composer listed above married his mentor's daughter?

B. Though she never composed an opera herself, Nadia Boulanger's pupils included such opera composers as Glass, Copland, and Thomson. With which composer listed above had she herself studied composition?

C. When Fauré was a student, he was "big-brothered" by a piano master only ten years older than him who, like Fauré, went on to compose a handful of operas. Who was he?

31. SOUND EFFECTS

The language spoken in the land of Gilbert and Sullivan's *Utopia, Limited* is a string of nonsense syllables. Luckily, the characters in the operetta wish to emulate the British and confine most of their speech and songs to English! But even better-known works by that same composer-lyricist team contain nonsense rhymes. Can you identify the shows these come from?

1. "Toi the riddle, loi the riddle, lol lol lay"
2. "Tantantara! Tzing! Boom!"
3. "Trial-la-law"
4. "Hey willow waly o"
5. "Sing hey! Sing holly, tolly! Sorry for some!"
6. "Sing hey, lackaday"
7. "Heighaly! Heighaly!" Misery me, lackalaydee!"

8. "Ah, well-a-day!"
9. "Tarantara! Tarantara!"
10. "Taradiddle, taradiddle—Toi lol lay!"
11. "Alalah! Alalah! Willahalah! Willaloo! Willahalah! Willaloo!"
12. "Tantantarara-rara-rara!"
13. "Ulahlica! Ulahlica! Ulahlica!"
14. "Etoia! Etoia! Opoponax! Etoia!"
15. "Fol diddle, lol diddle, lol lol lay"

Extra Credit:

A. Whose entrance line in *Utopia, Limited* is "Lalabalele talala! Callabale lalabalica folahle"?

B. What does he say when he *really* wants to let off steam?

C. What optional character was specially created by Gilbert to come in to take the lowest note of the Madrigal in *The Mikado* in case Pish-Tush's voice did not extend so deeply?

32. A MUSICAL MINORITY, PART I

Without even touching *Otello* or *L'Africaine* (the latter of which is really about a Hindu woman!), the writer of this book easily collected material enough for these quizzes about black singers, composers, and lyricists, or works concerning black culture. Start here...

1. On whose novel was *Porgy and Bess* based?

2. Who was the first man to perform the role of Porgy?

3. Who was his first Bess?

4. In the 1959 film of the opera, what actor (dubbed by a singer) played Porgy?

5. In that film what actress, similarly dubbed by a singer, played Bess?

6. At the time of this printing, why must nearly every role in *Porgy and Bess* be performed by black artists?

7. What does Truman Capote's "The Muses Are Heard" have to do with this opera?

8. Who was the first black woman to sing a principal role at the Met?

9. What was it?

10. Who was the first black man to sing a principal role at the Met?

11. What was it?

12. Kurt Weill's *Street Scene* employed a black lyricist. Who?

13. In the list of roles in *Street Scene* is a black janitor who is given his own blues number. What is the man's name?

14. What was the inaugural production of Opera Ebony, founded in 1976?

15. One of the company's founders was a mezzo-turned-nun. Who was she?

Extra Credit:

Name the professional debut roles of the following opera singers:

A. Willard White
B. Grace Bumbry
C. Jessye Norman
D. Leona Mitchell
E. Curtis Rayam
F. Barbara Hendricks

33. A MUSICAL MINORITY, PART II

1. What opera, which had its world premiere at New York City Opera, concerns a black slave accused of witchcraft?

2. What opera is based upon Alan Paton's *Cry, the Beloved Country?*

3. In what country is the opera set?

4. What Menotti opera is set in an African forest?

5. In what Verdi opera is a half-Incan character discriminated against and called a mulatto?

6. In what opera does a black Pullman porter become the emperor of an island in the West Indies?

7. Whose play is this work based on?

8. What white singer created the title role of this opera…in blackface?

9. Where was Scott Joplin born?

10. What is his only extant opera?

11. What is the origin of the character's title name, as explained in the course of the opera?

12. What do the conjurers in that work try to sell to people?

13. What Philip Glass opera features Martin Luther King as a leading figure?

14. What French opera, which premiered in 1856, features an aria sung by a slave on an American plantation?

15. To avoid political friction, a Brazilian opera originally about the liberation of African slaves was changed to concern Native Americans. What work is this?

Extra Credit:

A. What opera company produced the first North American staging of the opera of question 15, in 1989?

B. For whom did Gershwin compose the role of Porgy, but he turned it down?

C. What other Joplin opera existed long enough to be copyrighted, but has never been found?

34. A MUSICAL MINORITY, PART III

1. What Carlisle Floyd opera includes a quartet sung by black children celebrating the defeat of the Confederates?

2. What principal character of the above opera is revealed to be a member of the Ku Klux Klan?

3. In what 1977 opera do black characters sing "Burn, baby, burn!"?

4. What was the first American opera composed for an all-black cast?

5. Where is its action set?

6. What is the name of the quadroon slave in Victor Herbert's *Naughty Marietta?*

7. In *Show Boat,* what character is accused of being black and is thereby forbidden to act in shows on the work's vessel?

8. What British composer wrote an opera about Harriet Tubman?

9. What opera concerns the Haitian slaves' revolt against the French?

10. What black composer wrote it?

11. What is the name of the slaves' leader, a character based upon a genuine historical figure?

12. Who composed an opera about the life of Malcolm X?

13. Who wrote its libretto?

14. Who created its title role at the opera's world premiere?

15. What black soprano sang the role of Cleopatra in the Met's opening night performance in *Giulio Cesare?*

Extra Credit:

A. What nineteenth-century tenor earned the nickname "the black Mario" (after Italian tenor Giovanni Mario)?

B. What soprano was dubbed "the black Patti" and went on to name her own opera troupe after that?

C. Who was the first black opera singer to appear in a white American opera company?

35. SHIPSHAPE

While opera usually takes place onstage, some operas take place on ships, or otherwise concern floating vessels.

1. Outside which town is the *H.M.S. Pinafore* anchored?

2. What must Idomeneo sacrifice to Neptune in return for being saved from a sea storm?

3. What is the name of Jake's boat in *Porgy and Bess?*

4. What enemy land is spotted by the crew during *Billy Budd?*

5. What body of water must William Tell cross to reach his home, in Act IV of Rossini's opera?

6. What is the name of Sadko's ship?

7. What is the name of the frigate that sinks in *Candide?*

8. In the "Boston" version of *Un Ballo in Maschera,* what is the name of the sailor who "gets lucky"?

9. In *Il Pirata,* Itulbo claims to be the captain of a ship from what foreign state?

10. What is the name of the brigantine in *La Gioconda?*

11. Where was Isabella headed, in *L'Italiana in Algeri,* when her boat was shipwrecked?

12. What is the name of the performance vessel in *Show Boat?*

13. In what bay does Daland's boat drop anchor as *Der Fliegende Holländer* opens?

14. What Gilbert and Sullivan character appears in both *H.M.S. Pinafore* and *Utopia Limited?*

15. In what opera does an aria *"Cielo e mar"* ("Sky and sea") appear?

Extra Credit:

A. After what genuine ship was the original stage set of *H.M.S. Pinafore* modeled?

B. What was Gilbert's first choice for that operetta's name?

C. In *The Pirates of Penzance,* Frederic is praised for his skill at attacking vessels of what two companies?

36. MET OBSCURITY

While the Met stands for fame, it didn't help these operas very much. All were performed by that company less than ten times apiece. Can you name their better known composers?

1. *Il Matrimonio Segreto*
2. *Die Aegyptische Helena*
3. *Saint Elizabeth*
4. *La Wally*
5. *Don Quichotte*
6. *Linda di Chamounix*
7. *Manru*
8. *Mireille*
9. *Phoebus and Pan*
10. *Prince Igor*
11. *L'Heure Espagnole*
12. *Dinorah*
13. *La Vestale*
14. *La Campana Sommersa*
15. *Amelia Goes to the Ball*

Extra Credit:

A. What three operas were performed at the Met exactly once?

B. What opera, generally considered part of standard repertory, was—as of this printing—performed less than five times at the Met (back in 1916!)?

C What opera, given at the Met in 1891, was composed by Ernest II, the Duke of Saxe-Coburg?

37. PRIZE SONGS

In contrast to those losers of the last quiz, now let's have some winners!

1. In what year were the Metropolitan Opera National Auditions established?

2. What singer won the first Marian Anderson Award?

3. Who was the first recipient of the first official Richard Tucker Award?

4. The Luciano Pavarotti International Voice Competition is associated with what opera company?

5. What do the following singers have in common with respect to a New York City–based singing competition:
   Dawn Upshaw   Stanford Olsen
   Barbara Hendricks   Jan Opalach

6. What was the first opera to win a Pulitzer Prize for music?

7. What opera composer won the first Pulitzer Prize for music, though not for an opera?

8. For what opera did Robert Ward win a Pulitzer Prize?

9. Who was the first singer to win the Metropolitan Opera National Auditions' Birgit Nilsson Prize?

10. Who was the first singer to receive *Musical America*'s "Musician of the Year" award?

Extra Credit:

A. Who is the only composer to win two Pulitzer Prizes for operas, and what are their titles?

B. What two singers won the very first Metropolitan Opera National Auditions?

C. The Yapi Kredi International Leyla Gencer Voice Competition was inaugurated in 1995. Where was it held?

38. WETTING THEIR WHISTLES

Not all operatic characters are teetotalers, as this list of beverages named onstage goes to show. Match each liquor to the opera in which it is mentioned.

1. *Wein der Sim*   a. *Der Rosenkavalier*
2. *Manzanilla*   b. *Arabella*
3. *Marsimino*   c. *Francesca da Rimini*
4. *Un bottaglia di Xeres*   d. *La Jolie Fille de Perth*

5. Tokay
6. *Un demigiana di Cipro*
7. *Du vieux whisky d'Ecosse*
8. *Montrachet*
9. Elderberry wine
10. *Vino di Scio*
11. *Romanee-Conti*
12. Moët-Chandor
13. *Benediktiner*
14. Madeira
15. *Viel Sekt*

e. *Vanessa*
f. *Don Giovanni*
g. *Die Fledermaus*
h. *Der Fliegende Holländer*
i. *Lulu*
j. *Carmen*
k. *Falstaff*
l. *Regina*

Extra Credit:

A. In *Lucrezia Borgia,* four regional wines are served at the party at the Princess Negroni's. What are they, and which has been poisoned by the title character?

B. In what work do several characters compare the virtues of *xérès, malaga,* madeira, *alicante,* and port?

C. In what Offenbach operetta is a character dubbed Baron de Vermout von Bock-bier, Comte d'Avali-vintt-Katt-schopp-Ver-giss Mein-nicht?

39. DIRECT THE DONS

Not one a Donald, each "Don" on the left appears in a work named at right. Can you help them find their correct operas?

1. Don Antonio
2. Don Carlos
3. Don Fernando
4. Don Ramiro
5. Don Pedro
6. Don Marco
7. Don Cassandro
8. Don Diego
9. Don Andronico
10. Don Magnifico

a. *Betrothal in a Monastery*
b. *La Finta Semplice*
c. *Béatrice et Bénédict*
d. *Don Giovanni*
e. *Il Turco in Italia*
f. *Fidelio*
g. *Così Fan Tutte*
h. *Ernani*
i. *Carmen*
j. *La Cenerentola*

11. Don Narciso	k. *The Saint of Bleecker Street*
12. Don Ottavio	l. *La Forza del Destino*
13. Don Alvaro	m. *Il Guarany*
14. Don José	n. *Don Procopio*
15. Don Alfonso	

Extra Credit:

A. What is another name for the Verdian character Ernani?

B. What Purcell opera is based upon the adventures of Don Juan?

C. In New York City Opera's roster during the 1960s through the 1980s, there was a man whose actual name was Don Carlo. What position did he have with the company?

40. THE EASTERN SHUTTLE

Once outside the familiar boundaries of France, Italy, and Germany, most operagoers' memories begin to go a little blurry. Can you match these composers—all from Eastern European countries—to their operas?

1. Bartók	a. *Kátya Kabanová*
2. Erkel	b. *Duke Bluebeard's Castle*
3. Dvořák	c. *Julietta*
4. Janáček	d. *Dalibor*
5. Kodaly	e. *Rusalka*
6. Smetana	f. *Halka*
7. Penderecki	g. *King Roger*
8. Martinů	h. *Háry János*
9. Szymanowski	i. *Hunyady László*
10. Moniuszko	j. *The Devils of Loudon*

Extra Credit:

A. *Duke Bluebeard's Castle* is said to have been influenced by a Viennese work with which it has been performed as a double-bill. Name the other opera.

B. Of the ten men above, which composer's last operatic work is an unfinished adaptation of Shakespeare's *Twelfth Night*, called *Viola?*

C. What Janáček opera is based upon Dostoyevsky's prison diaries?

41. COUNTDOWN

Got your calculator ready? Match these ten operas to their composers.

1.	*1000 Airplanes on the Roof*	a.	Paulus
2.	*Nine Rivers from Jordan*	b.	Wolf-Ferrari
3.	*The Seven Deadly Sins*	c.	Martín y Soler
4.	*Six Characters in Search of an Author*	d.	Smetana
5.	*I Quattro Rusteghi*	e.	Weisgall
6.	*The Threepenny Opera*	f.	Glass
7.	*The Two Widows*	g.	Offenbach
8.	*Les Deux Aveugles*	h.	Weill
9.	*The Postman Always Rings Twice*		
10.	*Una Cosa Rara*		

Extra Credit:

A. In what Verdi opera is a man named Jacopo exiled by the Council of Ten?

B. What two composers created *Die Drei Pintos?*

C. How many operatic acts are in *Four Saints in Three Acts?*

42. EARLY AMERICAN OPERA

How much do you know about the "roots" of American opera? Take this quiz and find out.

1. What is considered the first American opera?

2. Who was the only composer to sign the Declaration of Independence?

3. What was the first foreign-language opera to be performed in its original language in North America?

4. What impressario was instrumental in presenting the American premieres of *Aida, Carmen, Rigoletto,* and other works?

5. What was the first American opera based upon a native literary source?

6. What was the first grand opera composed in the United States?

7. During the first few decades of the nineteenth-century, what city was considered the opera capital of the U.S.?

8. Under whose management did the "Swedish Nightingale," Jenny Lind, come to America?

9. Who is the first American composer to have had a work commissioned by the Met?

10. What was it?

Extra Credit:

A. Who was the first American-born woman to sing in a Wagnerian opera in the U.S.?

B. The only opera by Mrs. H. A. A. (Amy) Beach concerns the War of 1812. What is its title?

C. What was the first opera performed by the Juilliard School, in 1929?

43. TAKE A CHANCE

Opera often concerns gambling. What are your chances of answering the following?

1. What game do Tabor's cronies play during Act II of *The Ballad of Baby Doe?*

2. At what game does Guillot accuse the Chevalier des Grieux of cheating?

3. What card game is played in Act I of *La Fanciulla del West?*

4. In *McTeague,* who wins the lottery?

5. With what hand does Minnie win her card game with Jack Rance?

6. What number do the dice players in *Porgy and Bess* want to come up?

7. When the ladies have their fortunes told in *Carmen,* how many cards does Frasquita have read?

8. Who tells Herman the three cards that will win for him in *The Queen of Spades?*

9. What game is in progress as the curtain comes up on *Fedora?*

10. When Robert le Diable has no more money with which to play at dice, what does he stake to continue playing?

11. Why does the Prince of Granada win the jousting tournament, without even jousting, in *Robert le Diable?*

12. What card game is played by Stroh and his cronies in *Intermezzo?*

13. At what game do people gamble in *La Gioconda?*

14. How much do Ferrando and Guglielmo bet that Dorabella and Fiordiligi will be faithful to them?

15. At what German spa does Prokofiev's *The Gambler* take place?

Extra Credit:

A. In *Albert Herring,* Sid bets Albert double or nothing the price of his purchases at the greengrocer's. Had Albert accepted the bet and won, how much would Sid have had to pay up?

B. In what Italian opera are the words "Dooda, dooda, day"—from "Camptown Races"—sung onstage?

C. During the gambling match between the Chevalier des Grieux and Guillot, upon whom do Poussette and Javotte bet?

44. WE *ARE* AMUSED

Can you match each composer at left with a famous personage at right from whom he enjoyed special favor? (Several have more than one answer.)

1. Cimarosa		a. Henry IV
2. Paisiello		b. Louis XIV
3. Spontini		c. Charles X
4. Cavalli		d. Catherine II
5. Lully		e. Queen Anne
6. Peri		f. Emperor Leopold II
7. Mozart		g. Napoleon
8. Handel		h. Louis XVIII
9. Rossini		i. Napoleon III
10. Auber		j. Emperor Joseph II

Extra Credit:

A. Haydn composed *Arianna Abbandonada* to showcase a soprano said to be the mistress of the Prince of Wales. Who was she?

B. When Beaumarchais's play *Le Barbier de Séville* was performed in a private production, the queen of France herself took the role of Rosina. Who was her husband?

C. What Gilbert and Sullivan operetta was given at Windsor for Queen Victoria?

45. A MUSICAL MENAGERIE

In spite of one or two predatory titles such as *Der Wildschütz* (The Poacher), opera boasts a number of works named for animals. Can you match these to their composers?

1. *The Bear*		a.	Puccini
2. *Le Coq d'Or*		b.	Mozart
3. *La Rondine*		c.	Beeson
4. *Baa Baa Black Sheep*		d.	Floyd
5. *Die Englische Katz*		e.	Rossini
6. *L'Oca del Cairo*		f.	Auber
7. *The Cunning Little Vixen*		g.	Offenbach
8. *Captain Jinks of the Horse Marines*		h.	Britten
		i.	Walton
9. *La Gazza Ladra*		j.	Henze
10. *Le Docteur Ox*		k.	Rimsky-Korsakov
11. *The White Horse Inn*		l.	Moore
12. *Albert Herring*		m.	Janáček
13. *The Wings of a Dove*		n.	Benatzky
14. *Of Mice and Men*		o.	Berkeley
15. *Le Cheval de Bronze*			

Extra Credit:

A. What creepy operatic character sings an "Aria of the Worm"?

B. What French operetta about a dog was dubbed a...female dog...by the press?

C. What two composers created *L'Aiglon* ("The Eaglet")?

46. AT THE MOVIES, PART I

Fans of opera movies and videos will get these in a flick of a moment.

1. How many Academy Awards did *Amadeus* win?

2. Who conducted the score of the Zeffirelli movie *Otello?*

3. What Belgian bass-baritone starred in *The Music Teacher?*

4. Who conducted the Zeffirelli film *La Traviata?*

5. What Fellini movie concerns the funeral voyage of an opera star?

6. What film cast Klaus Kinski as a man obsessed with building an opera house in the Amazon?

7. Who played the throat therapist who fell for Pavarotti in *Yes, Giorgio?*

8. Who directed the 1984 film *Carmen* starring Domingo?

9. *Wagner,* starring Richard Burton, was originally a nine-hour British TV series. As a movie, how long does it run?

10. What movie, featuring Cher, contains several numbers from *La Bohème?*

11. What Vietnam film incorporates Wagner's "Ride of the Valkyries" into its score?

12. What Jack Nicholson movie contains *"Nessun dorma"* in its score?

13. What is the title of the documentary of Pavarotti's 1986 trip to China?

14. What opera is Dudley Moore shown conducting in the movie *Foul Play?*

15. The opera sets for the above scene belonged to another opera. Name it.

Extra Credit:

Name all ten directors of the multipart film *Aria.*

47. AT THE MOVIES, PART II

And here are some more recent developments:

1. In *Diva,* what opera singer portrays the eponymous role?

2. What aria appears in the film as a kind of leitmotif?

3. In *Pretty Woman*, what opera does Richard Gere take Julia Roberts to see?

4. The 1992 film *In the Shadow of the Stars* concerns the chorus of which opera company?

5. What Oscar did it win?

6. What 1991 film stars Glenn Close as a diva?

7. Who was dubbed in as her voice?

8. The film concerns a conductor's desire to produce a particular opera. Name the opera.

9. In 1994, Gérard Corbeau directed a movie about a legendary singer. What was it called?

10. In honor of Jean Cocteau, an American composer has created a trilogy of mixed-format theatrical works, the centerpiece of which is an opera meant to be heard concurrently with a (silent) screening of the classic film *La Belle et la Bête*. Who is this composer?

11. The 1996 French film *Madame Butterfly* (filmed in Tunisia!) stars what Chinese opera singer as Cio-Cio-San?

12. Name the 1991 movie about Beethoven.

13. Who plays Ludwig?

14. A 1986 Swedish comedy is about an avant-garde production by a Stockholm opera company. Name the film.

15. Name the opera.

Extra Credit:

A. Westerners may learn much about the training of youngsters for Chinese opera in what 1995 movie?

B. In that film, who plays Dieyi, the gay male singer of female roles?

C. A 1993 film also concerns Chinese opera. What is its title?

48. VINTAGE OPERA FILMS

Were the questions in the last quizzes a little too modern for you? Here's a quiz for old-movie buffs.

1. In what 1935 movie did Lawrence Tibbett play a struggling opera singer?

2. In what 1936 movie was Jeanette MacDonald's costar Clark Gable?

3. What was the first movie to pair up Jeanette MacDonald and Nelson Eddy?

4. Allan Jones and Mary Martin starred in what 1939 movie about a famous operetta composer?

5. In what 1948 movie did Jarmila Novotná play a mother looking for her lost son?

6. What 1938 movie about an operetta composer won an Oscar for Best Cinematography?

7. What soprano was showcased in that film?

8. In what 1952 movie did Mario Lanza play an opera singer who got drafted?

9. Kirsten Flagstad costarred with W. C. Field and Dorthy Lamour—among others—in what movie?

10. Deanna Durbin sang *"Musetta's Waltz"* and *"Ave Maria"* in what 1940 movie?

11. What Durbin film won an Oscar in 1937 for Best Musical Score?

12. What was unusual about Tito Gobbi's casting in the 1951 film of *Pagliacci?*

13. Lily Pons, Henry Fonda, and Lucille Ball appeared together in what 1935 film?

14. What 1930 movie includes a recital by John McCormack?

15. Who played the title role in the 1935 film *Mimi,* based on *La Bohème?*

Extra Credit:

The 1951 British film *Tales of Hoffman* (sic) was expertly dubbed by opera singers, its onscreen cast largely composed of actors and ballet dancers. Who supplied the voices for the following roles:

A. Lindorf
B. Nicklausse
C. Olympia
D. Giulietta
E. and F. And who both acted and sang two principal roles themselves?

49. KEEPING COUNT

Specific numbers come up in the course of many operas. How good are you at musical arithmetic?

1. Minnie asks Billy Jackrabbit to count to a certain number. What is it?

2. How long was Don José's prison sentence for letting Carmen escape?

3. How many years have Fiorilla and Don Geronio been married?

4. How many kisses does Tosca promise she will give Cavaradossi after his mock execution is over?

5. At the start of *La Traviata*, how long has the Baron known Violetta?

6. How long has Alfredo secretly been in love with her?

7. How many years was the Dutchman's term at sea?

8. How many years had Augusta Tabor been married to Horace before she discovered his affair with Baby Doe?

9. How many years pass between the Prologue and Act I of *Simon Boccanegra?*

10. Ping mocks the deaths of Turandot's suitors, singing that one would be better off with a harem than with one Turandot. How many wives does he advocate that a man should take?

11. How long did Mandryka have the picture of Arabella before coming to woo her?

12. For how many years does Falstaff claim that he has helped Bardolfo in food and drink in Verdi's opera?

13. How many locks are on the chest stored in the Cave of Hercules in *Don Rodrigo?*

14. How many years of servitude does Caspar still owe to Samiel at the start of *Der Freischütz?*

15. What opera begins with two characters comparing notes on how many cars, planes, houses, and wives they have?

Extra Credit:

A. In what opera does an elderly mathematician sing a song about multiplication and the metric system?

B. According to the original stage directions, what number forms his hat?

C. What Gilbert and Sullivan character boasts about his expertise in calculus?

50. MUSICAL NOTES

Opera texts, not surprisingly, sometimes concern music.

1. In what opera are the composers Gluck, Lully, Rameau, Piccinni, and Couperin mentioned?

2. What two Richard Strauss operas are also name-dropped in the above works?

3. In what French opera are the French operas *Manon, Mignon,* and *Pré de Clerc* (sic) discussed?

4. What is the name of the onstage pianist in *Fedora?*

5. What operetta—about a fictional composer's need to supply a new waltz for a show—is based upon a motion picture released three years earlier?

6. In what opera does the main character exclaim at the sight of the work's genuine composer on a television screen?

7. In what opera is critic Andrew Porter mentioned?

8. In what non-French opera is a French song played on an offstage phonograph?

9. In the original production and traditional stagings of the above opera, whose voice is on the record?

10. Who is said to have been the composer of the song that the Marquise of Berkenfield wants Marie to sing?

11. In what operetta does the cast include a female conductor of a ladies' orchestra?

12. What is the name of the opera within Britten's *Let's Make an Opera?*

13. In what German opera do the ghosts of nine composers appear to the title character?

14. In what opera does a composer demonstrate the "electrododecaphonic" style of music?

15. What American opera concerns a composer who drowned in Lake Como?

Extra Credit:

A. In what Rossini opera are Haydn, Mozart, Beethoven, and Bach praised for their use of syncopation?

B. What is the name of the composer who is introduced to the guests at the Act I ball in *Andrea Chénier* along with the title character?

C. What is the name of the performance venue in *Zazà?*

51. RECYCLED ROSSINI

It's a well-known fact that Rossini was no slouch when it came to reusing his own compositions. How many Rossinian "roots" can you identify?

1. *"O fiamma soave,"* the tenor aria from *La Donna del Lago,* is set to a tune from what other opera?

2. Cenerentola's *"Non più mesta accanto al fuoco"* reuses music from what rarely performed tenor aria?

3. The tenor Comte Ory's *"Que les destins prospères"* was originally written for a soprano in what opera?

4. The cabaletta from a duet in what opera reappears in the Osiris-Pharaoh duet in *Mosè in Egitto?*

5. The famous overture to *Il Barbiere di Siviglia* had its first hearing in what opera?

6. For which other opera did Rossini recycle it?

7. For the Milan production of *L'Italiana in Algeri,* Rossini wrote a new tenor aria called *"Concedi, amor pietoso"* to replace *"Oh, come il cor di giubilo."* From what aria had he lifted the "new" cabaletta?

8. An alternative cavatina for the soprano in *Il Turco in Italia* reappears in a slightly different form in what other comic opera?

9. Part of *"Una voce poco fa"* was first used in what opera seria as the entrance aria of its title character?

10. *Il Viaggio a Reims*'s "Gran Pezza Concertato a 14 Voci" was installed in the Act I finale of what opera?

11. The music for the Rossini-Figaro duet was first heard in what opera. Name it.

12. The Act I finale of *Il Barbiere di Siviglia* was drawn from yet another opera. Name it.

13. The music for Berta's *"Il vecchiotto cerca moglie"* comes from what opera?

14. Almaviva's *"Ecco ridente in cielo"* was originally a piece for chorus in what opera?

15. In *La Pietra del Paragone,* Clarice's cavatina *"Eco pietosa tu sei la sola"* suspiciously resembles music from what opera seria?

Extra Credit:

Some of Rossini's lesser-known operas have interesting alternative names.

A. What is the "or" subtitle of *Matilde di Shabran?*

B. What is the "or" subtitle of *Moïse et Pharaon?*

C. What Rossini opera was performed à la P. G. Wodehouse in 1996 by England's Hatstand Opera as *Love's Luggage Lost?*

52. OPERA IN GREAT BRITAIN

How much do you know about your English-speaking fellow opera-lovers across the sea?

1. What is London's largest opera house?

2. What is the former name of the English National Opera?

3. What distinguishes the troupe from the Royal Opera, with regard to their repertoire?

4. What annual summer festival is held in Sussex?

5. On whose estate is it held?

6. Who was the first artistic director of the Edinburgh Festival?

7. How many theaters in London have been called Covent Garden?

8. When was Covent Garden's resident opera company given the title "Royal Opera"?

9. What opera inaugurated the Royal English Opera House, now known as the Palace Theatre?

10. What is considered the first English opera?

11. What titled opera-lover founded *Opera* magazine in 1950?

12. In what British opera production were "scratch and sniff" cards distributed for audience participation?

13. What national-level company is based in Leeds?

14. What national-level company is based in Cardiff?

15. On 5/28/94, a new opera house opened at the site of question 4, with which opera that had inaugurated the old house exactly sixty years earlier?

Extra Credit:

A. Who founded the Aldeburgh festival, and why is it held at that site?

B. What briefly existent opera troupe, organized by and named for a famous conductor, produced Russian operas using sets left behind when the Diaghilev Company fled England at the start of World War I?

C. On what English politician do historians believe the character of Macheath in *The Beggar's Opera* was based?

53. THE INN SPOTS

Each of the restaurants, inns, hotels, and taverns at left features in an opera at right. Can you match them up?

1. Windsor Hotel	a. *Andrea Chénier*
2. Boar	b. *La Rondine*
3. The Golden Lily	c. *La Périchole*
4. Grundslee Inn	d. *La Fanciulla del West*
5. Tiro	e. Auber's *Manon Lescaut*
6. Polka	f. *Intermezzo*
7. Clarendon Hotel	g. *Peter Grimes*
8. Willard Hotel	h. *Werther*
9. Café Hottot	i. *The Ballad of Baby Doe*
10. The Three Cousins	j. *Fedora*
11. Palmetto	k. *Falstaff*

12. The Blue Dial
13. The Golden Grape
14. Bancelin's
15. Garter Inn

Extra Credit:

A. What five establishments are recommended as places that Ruggero should visit, in *La Rondine?*

B. In what opera does an unnamed inn bear a sign that translates to "Good lodging for good money"?

C. In what inn hangs a sign with the motto *"Hony soit qui mal y pense"?*

54. COLD CASH

If you think ticket prices are high, look at the kind of money that changes hands during opera performances!

1. What bribe does Cavaradossi promise the jailor in return for delivering a letter to Tosca?

2. How much does Pinkerton owe Goro for Butterfly?

3. What amount does Gianni Schicchi allow for funeral expenses?

4. How much has the painting of Lulu as a dancer sold for?

5. How much does Nemorino pay for his love philtre?

6. How much does Porgy give Frazier for Bess's "divorce" from Crown?

7. What does Billy Jackrabbit pay Wowkle's father in order to marry her?

8. How much does Don Giovanni pay Leporello to swap places with him?

9. What is Abdul's payment for pretending to be a caveman in *The Last Savage?*

10. What bill does Norina ring up while buying hats after her "marriage" to Don Pasquale?

11. How much does the Chevalier des Grieux inherit from his mother?

12. What does Ochs demand as compensation besides his dowry?

13. What is Basilio's payment for witnessing Almaviva's marriage to Rosina?

14. What is the opera troupe's payment for performing "Ariadne" in *Ariadne auf Naxos?*

15. Who proposes to present a bill to Parliament levying a tax on fat people?

Extra Credit:

A. Who shows off a framed dollar—the first he earned—to his daughter's suitor?

B. In what opera do the characters take up a collection for a man's funeral by dropping money into a saucer on the deceased man's chest?

C. Who composed the operetta *Die Dollarprinzessin?*

55. BOOKWORMS

Some operatic characters display their cultural depth by making references to literary works or legends. Match the names at left to the operas in which they are mentioned.

1. Tristan and Isolde	a. *Fedora*
2. Otello and Iago	b. *Capriccio*
3. Don Juan and Elvira	c. *Don Quichotte*
4. Roxane	d. *L'Elisir d'Amore*
5. El Cid	e. *Manon Lescaut*
6. Prince Charming and	f. *Chérubin*
Sleeping Beauty	g. *Francesca da Rimini*

7. The Fox (and the
   Grapes)
8. Pandora
9. Orlando Furioso
10. Lancelot (Galeotto) and
    Guenevere

h. *Louise*
i. *La Serva Padrona*

Extra Credit:

A. What opera includes recited excerpts from *Frommer's Guide to Egypt* and *Fodor's Egypt?*

B. In what German opera is Pascal quoted?

C. Wiliam Blake and Oscar Wilde are quoted in what American opera?

56. SONGFEST

Each of the songs at left does not appear in any opera, but—often sung in soloist recitals—was penned by an opera composer at right. Match them up.

1. *"Les filles de Cadix"*
2. *"Ouvre tes yeux bleus"*
3. *"Clair de lune"*
4. "Suleika"
5. *"Er ist's"*
6. *"Le spectre de la rose"*
7. *"La flute enchantée"*
8. *"Ballade des gros dindons"*
9. "None but the Lonely Heart"
10. *"La danza"*
11. *"Warnung"*
12. *"Chanson d'avril"*
13. "The Lost Chord"
14. *"Zueignung"*
15. *"Si mes vers avaient des ailes!"*

a. Hahn
b. Bizet
c. Strauss
d. Tchaikovsky
e. Debussy
f. Ravel
g. Rossini
h. Schubert
i. Mozart
j. Berlioz
k. Sullivan
l. Chabrier
m. Schumann
n. Delibes
o. Massenet

Extra Credit:

What twentieth-century composers wrote the following song cycles?

A. "Knoxville, Summer of 1915"

B. "The Holy Sonnets of John Donne"

C. "Songfest"

57. SILVER NOTES AMONG THE GOLD

These opera composers all lived past eighty. How old were they on their final birthdays?

1. Camille Saint-Saëns
2. Ralph Vaughan Williams
3. Gustave Charpentier
4. Pietro Mascagni
5. Luigi Cherubini
6. Virgil Thomson
7. Richard Strauss
8. Giuseppe Verdi
9. Igor Stravinsky
10. Darius Milhaud

Extra Credit:

A. At what age did tenor Hugues Cuénod make his Met debut?

B. What opera, by then eighty-four-year-old Sir Michael Tippett, had its world premiere at the Houston Grand Opera in 1989?

C. What conductor led his first *Ring,* with the Seattle Opera, at the age of eighty-two?

58. HIGH FASHION

Costume, of course, bears a great deal of importance in opera. How fashion-conscious are you?

1. For whom does Porgy buy a hat trimmed with feathers?

2. What comic opera concerns a pair of identical hats?

3. To what article of clothing does the ribbon that Cherubino steals belong?

4. Who goes to pieces when her clothing trunks are destroyed in a coach accident?

5. Who sings an aria called *"Quella del velo"*—a song about a veil?

6. In what opera does the leading character request a black wedding veil?

7. What operatic character is supposed to remain veiled until she is twenty?

8. How does Emilia obtain Desdemona's handkerchief in Verdi's *Otello?*

9. In what opera is the dropping of a royal crown taken as a terrifying omen?

10. In what opera does a shoe salesman describe his wares?

11. Who becomes angry when her father tells her to sew a plain gown for herself because her stepmother has just bought a new, expensive dress?

12. Where does Fedora hide and carry a fatal dose of poison?

13. In what opera does a woman, envious of another's gown, demand that her party guests do a fast dance that will make them perspire so that when the ladies retire to change into dry clothing, she may swipe the dress and put it on herself?

14. What does Dulcinée ask Don Quichotte to retrieve from a bandit in Massenet's opera?

15. What early nineteenth-century opera requires one of its performers to wear black armor with the visor down?

Extra Credit:

A. As has been documented in several autobiographies, Beverly Sills once cut up a costume rather than wear it, because she felt its color didn't suit her. What opera was it for?

B. During the 10/24/87 New York City Opera performance of *Tosca,* what soprano in the title role caught her heavy gown on a staircase and had to sing part of Act I tethered to the scenery until a member of the company cut her free?

C. In recent years, the Met production of a certain opera has dressed the orchestra and conductor in casual clothing for the first half of the work, and formal wear for the balance of the show. What opera is it?

59. WHAT'S IN A NAME

How keenly have you listened to the name-dropping that occurs in opera?

1. In what opera are the names "Sorenson," "Seligman," and "Sokoloff" heard?

2. Who are Madelon, Ninetta, Caton, Regina, Claretta, Violetta, Nerina, Ninon, and Georgetta, as a group?

3. What name did Dr. Schön give to Lulu?

4. What did Dr. Goll call her?

5. What is the name of the Italian tenor in *Capriccio?*

6. What is the name of Louise's father?

7. Whose second through sixth names are Maria Ehrenreich Bonaventura Ferdinand Hyacinth?

8. What is the Marschallin's nickname for Octavian?

9. What was Augusta Tabor's maiden name?

10. What is Captain Vere's full name?

11. By what name is Henry of Ofterdingen better known?

12. By what name does Louisa Miller's noble suitor call himself when he is disguised as a peasant?

13. What is the name of the maiden from whom Desdemona learned the "Willow Song"?

14. By what false names does Miss Pinkerton in *The Old Maid and the Thief* tell Bob to call himself?

15. Who is the bearer of the marriage contract of Don Pasquale and "Sofronia"?

Extra Credit:

A. Name Mandryka's three servants.

B. By what names are Ferrando and Guglielmo listed on the false marriage contract?

C. What four servants are called in to help toss Falstaff out the window when he is hidden in the laundry basket in Verdi's opera?

60. MARK YOUR CALENDARS

Can you supply the specific dates (degree of detail sometimes indicated in parentheses) to these items?

1. On what date (month/day/year) is Albert Herring chosen as King of the May?

2. What date (month/day/year) does the final scene in *X* depict?

3. What is the date (month/day/year) that the will is drawn up in *Gianni Schicchi?*

4. What is Frederic's birthday (month/day) in *The Pirates of Penzance?*

5. In what year will he turn twenty-one, by the pirates' reckoning?

6. In what year did Captain Vere command his ship, as described in *Billy Budd?*

7. In what year does *Arabella* take place?

8. On what date (month/day/year) does *Casanova* open?

9. In what month and year does Horace Tabor have his hallucinatory last scene in *The Ballad of Baby Doe?*

10. In what month and year does Act II of *Andrea Chénier* take place?

11. In what year is *La Muette de Portici* set?

12. On what date (month/day/year) does the investigation that occurs in *Miss Havisham's Fire* take place?

13. In what year is *La Juive* set?

14. In what year does Verdi's *Attila* take place?

15. In what year does *Regina* take place?

Extra Credit:

A. During what Chinese year were twelve suitors' heads chopped off in *Turandot?*

B. On what date (month/day/year) did Lady Billows's father shoot the otter whose pelt since became her purse?

C. What is the complete title of the operetta more commonly known as *Monsieur Choufleuri?*

61. SKIRTING THE ISSUE

"Pants roles"—women dressing up as men—are common to opera. More rarely does the reverse occur.

1. What name does Octavian take when disguised as a woman?

2. What name does le Comte Ory take when he dresses as a nun?

3. In *Daphne,* who disguises himself as a woman in order to win the affection of the title character in a sisterly fashion?

4. In what Poulenc opera do a husband and wife exchange sexual roles?

5. How many children does the husband bear?

6. In *Mavra,* the title role is taken by what male character who is pretending to be a female cook?

7. How is he found out?

8. In what Donizetti one-act opera is a pushy stage mother played by a baritone?

9. In Act III of *Le Nozze di Figaro*, who is the one to reveal that the befrocked Cherubino is really a boy?

10. In what twentieth-century opera is there an opera-within-an-opera featuring a performer who is supposedly a castrato playing a woman—and the singer turns out to really be a woman?

11. In what Offenbach operetta are the women of the title portrayed by men?

12. In *Candide*, which male character is proposed to by a man while disguised as a woman?

13. In *The Love for Three Oranges*, what female role is sung by a bass?

14. In *Falstaff*, who dresses up to take Nanetta's place as Queen of the Fairies?

15. In *A Midsummer Night's Dream*, which of the rustic players performs the female role of Thisbe in their play?

Extra Credit:

A. In what modern American opera does a bisexual Russian prince perform a cabaret scene partially in drag?

B. In Act IV of *La Bohème*, when the four roommates dance together, who momentarily acts the part of a shy young maiden?

C. In Cavalli's *La Calisto*, which female role is played throughout by a man?

62. ANIMAL HOUSE

As anyone in theatrical circles knows, life backstage can sometimes resemble a zoo. Onstage...as well!

1. What animal does Don Magnifico dream about?

2. What animal is featured on Otello's emblem?

3. Whose menagerie includes a tiger, a bear, and a crocodile?

4. In what opera is an old dog taken away to be shot?

5. In what opera are lapdogs and parrots offered for sale?

6. What animal draws the traveling theater cart in *Pagliacci?*

7. What is the name of Mrs. Jones's dog in *Street Scene?*

8. Who says that animals never cheat on each other, but men are unfaithful?

9. In what opera does the leading tenor brag about how he killed a bear?

10. In what opera does the title character turn out to be an ape?

11. What turn-of-the-century composer, more famous for longer operettas, wrote a short work called *The Zoo?*

12. Edgardo rescued Lucia from an attack by what animal?

13. What is the name of Smithy's frog in *The Jumping Frog of Calaveras County?*

14. How does a gambler attempt to "fix" the frog-jumping match?

15. In what crossover work does an ensemble include the voices of two sheep and a lion?

Extra Credit:

A. What opera opens with the sacrifice of three steeds?

B. In what Britten opera does a chorus sing about a cow jumping over the moon?

C. In *Der Freischütz,* what is the name of the dog Ännchen's aunt once mistook for a ghost?

63. APPETIZERS

What do these fifteen works have in common?

1. *Ariadne auf Naxos*
2. *La Bohème*
3. *Otello*
4. *Elektra*
5. *Die Frau ohne Schatten*
6. *Susannah*
7. *Tosca*
8. *L'Amore dei Tre Re*
9. *La Serva Padrona*
10. *Pelléas et Mélisande*
11. *Salome*
12. *Wozzeck*
13. *Noyes Fludde*
14. *Oedipus Rex*
15. *Vanessa*

Extra Credit:

A. What composer is thought to be the first to develop the compositional style known as the "French Overture"?

B. Which operatic overture would Mahler sometimes shift to introduce Act II instead of Act I when he conducted this opera, so that latecomers wouldn't miss it?

C. For which of his works did Verdi compose, but then decide not to use, a new overture forty-six years after the opera's premiere?

64. SAINTS ALIVE!

Match the saints at the left to the operas in which they are mentioned or exist as a character. This is a tricky one: some saints appear in more than one opera, some operas have more than one saint, and some saints share names.

1. Michael
2. John
3. Rosalie
4. Genevieve
5. Augustine
6. Ignatius Loyola
7. Margaret
8. Valentine

a. *La Jolie Fille de Perth*
b. *Don Carlos*
c. *Mireille*
d. *Four Saints in Three Acts*
e. *Der Mond*
f. *Robert le Diable*
g. *Die Meistersinger von Nürnberg*

9. Just
10. Giles
11. Louis
12. Crispin
13. T(h)eresa
14. Peter
15. Agnes

h. *Grisélidis*
i. *La Vie Parisienne*
j. *Manon*
k. *Jeanne d'Arc au Bûcher*
l. *The Rake's Progress*
m. *Il Viaggio a Reims*

Extra Credit:

A. In what opera do several ladies run through a number of saints' names while trying to guess the name of a shy young stranger?

B. In what opera is there a character called St. Settlement?

C. In the mini-Met production of the traditionally all-black *Four Saints in Three Acts,* what tenor was the only white principal artist in the cast?

65. FATHER TIME

Certain events in opera take place at specific times. Can you give the hours when the following take place?

1. Don Carlo declares his love to Eboli, thinking she is Elisabetta.
2. Violetta awakens in her bedroom.
3. Curtain time for the play in *Pagliacci.*
4. When Nedda plans to meet Silvio.
5. Falstaff's appointed hour at the Oak of Herne.
6. The end of Act I of *Louise.*
7. The beginning of Act II of *Louise.*
8. Sid's planned date with Nancy, in *Albert Herring.*
9. The peddlers in *Lakmé* pack up and leave the marketplace.
10. Golaud's horse takes fright and throws him.
11. Golaud warns Pelléas to avoid Mélisande.
12. Dr. Malatesta's expected arrival.
13. When Olivier wishes to meet Madeleine.

14. Ourrias's boat sinks.
15. The portrait of Cuno fell and struck Agathe.

Extra Credit:

A. In *L'Heure Espagnole,* which two characters are hidden inside grandfather clocks?

B. From what time of morning to what time of night will Phoebe stay by Fairfax's side, or so she swears in *The Yeomen of the Guard?*

C. In *Falstaff,* during what period of day is Ford absent from home?

66. SPECIAL MENTION

Each person on the left never appears in the opera in which he or she is mentioned, yet each is the subject of a song within a work listed at right. Can you pair up the person to the operatic source? Note: one lucky lade is sung about in two operas.

1. Piquillo	a. *La Wally*
2. Fatima	b. *Don Pasquale*
3. Vilia	c. *Roberto Devereux*
4. Joe	d. *Monsieur Choufleuri*
5. Nerina	e. *La Périchole*
6. Riccardo	f. *Sapho*
7. Rosamunda	g. *Die Lustige Witwe*
8. Queen Mab	h. *Les Contes d'Hoffmann*
9. Robin	i. *Mireille*
10. Rosalinde	j. *La Traviata*
11. Kleinzach	k. *Peter Grimes*
12. Max de Sedlitz-Calembourg	l. *Roméo et Juliette*
13. Doretta	m. *Manon*
14. Pedro	n. *Le Jongleur de Notre-Dame*
15. Magali	o. *La Rondine*
	p. *La Grande-Duchesse de Gérolstein*

Extra Credit:

A. During what aria does the Duke of Mantua refer to himself as Gualtier?

B. In *Porgy and Bess,* who sings a song about "Ole Man Sorrow"?

C. In what opera is there a ragtime number about a woman called Aunt Dinah?

67. AN OPERATIC AVIARY

"Canary parts" aside, opera does contain a number of references to our feathered friends. How attentive were you to their species?

1. What bird does Max shoot in Act I of *Der Freischütz?*

2. What bird does Agathe dream about?

3. What bird do Susannah and her brother sing about, in *Susanna?*

4. In what Britten opera do the characters include a dove and a raven?

5. What bird is the subject of Antonia's first aria in *Les Contes d'Hoffmann?*

6. In what Offenbach operetta does a dove fly down from Mount Olympus with a message?

7. In what Gilbert and Sullivan operetta is the subject of an Aesop fable—a jackdaw in peacock's feathers—listed along with other ominous proverbial allusions?

8. In what opera does a character sing about a turtledove in a vulture's nest?

9. In *La Bohème,* what bird is said to have met its death from consuming parsley?

10. Which of her birds does Baba the Turk love best?

11. What birds fly out of the tower as Pelléas strokes Mélisande's hair?

12. In what crossover work is a bird's neck broken onstage?

13. What is the name of Richard's ship in *Ruddigore?*

14. Who gave King Dodon the Golden Cockerel?

15. In what Gilbert and Sullivan operetta is there a song about a cock who doesn't crow?

Extra Credit:

A. In what opera, otherwise performed in English, does a character sing about *"l'hirondelle," "la rossignol,"* and *"le corbeau"?*

B. In what opera do seven varieties of birds sing in a garden at midday?

C. In what opera does a fox incite chickens to revolt against a rooster?

68. OUCH!

Along with "indisposed" performers, opera has its fill of ailing characters.

1. What injury causes Baron Ochs to literally scream murder?

2. What treatment does Figaro demand from Dr. Bartolo, during the shaving scene in Rossini's opera?

3. Who sneezes several times during *L'Italiana in Algeri?*

4. What bel canto work contains a trio in which one character sneezes while another can't stop yawning?

5. In what opera do choristers and the leading tenor feign laryngitis in order to go on strike for better conditions at the theater at which they are engaged to sing?

6. What operetta includes an aria dubbed "The Migraine Song"?

7. In what operetta does the title character sing "The Seasick Song"?

8. What disease afflicts the city in *Death in Venice?*

9. What operatic character has been recovering from fractured ribs?

10. In what opera is a leading character wheeled in on a gurney, totally encased in a plaster cast?

11. What disease does Lulu catch while in prison?

12. When Gennaro has swallowed poison in *Lucrezia Borgia*, who gives him the antidote?

13. In a sometimes-cut aria in *Candide,* it is inferred that a certain disease caused Pangloss to require an artificial nose. What is it?

14. What poison do Ferrando and Guglielmo pretend to take?

15. Why does Susanna decline to keep the Countess's smelling salts for herself?

Extra Credit:

A. In the Peter Sellers staging of *Così Fan Tutte,* what celebrity does Despina pretend to be when she comes forth to "cure" Ferrando and Guglielmo?

B. What kind of doctor does Almaviva, disguised as a soldier, claim to be?

C. In what opera is a woodchopper passed off as a doctor?

69. FIRST PERSON

The opera personalities at left—sometimes with a little help from others—all have written books about themselves or their stage-related ideas. Can you match the writers to their works, listed at right?

1. Hermann Prey	a. *5,000 Nights at the Opera*
2. Renata Scotto	b. *Musical Chairs*
3. Plácido Domingo	c. *My Road to Opera*
4. Sir Rudolf Bing	d. *Subsequent*
5. Elisabeth Söderstrom	*Performances*

6. Jonathan Miller	e. *My First 40 Years*
7. Robert Merrill	f. *Findings*
8. Boris Goldovsky	g. *A Knight at the Opera*
9. Schuyler Chapin	h. *My Life in Pictures*
10. Leonard Bernstein	i. *More Than a Diva*
11. Birgit Nilsson	j. *Between Acts*
12. Frank Corsaro	k. *Reverberations*
13. Dietrich Fischer-Dieskau	l. *My Lord, What a*
14. Marian Anderson	*Morning*
15. Harold Prince	m. *First Night Fever*
	n. *Contradictions*
	o. *Maverick*
	p. *In My Own Key*

Extra Credit:

A. What then-member of the Metropolitan Opera House staff wrote *The Authentic Pasta Cookbook,* published in 1985?

B. What American bass has collected interviews with colleagues into a volume called *Great Singers on Great Singing?*

C. What are the titles of Beverly Sills's three published autobiographies?

70. STRANGER THAN TRUTH

There are also fictional accounts of the world of opera—several written by singers themselves. Can you match these books to their correct authors?

1. *Elegy for a Soprano*	a. Barbara Paul
2. *Diva*	b. William Lewis
3. *Prima Donna at Large*	c. Delacorta
4. *Cry to Heaven*	d. Robert Merrill (with
5. *The Hamster Opera*	Fred Jarvis)
Company	e. (editor) Thomas Godfrey
6. *Gala*	f. Anne Rice
7. *A Cadenza for Caruso*	g. Janis Mitchell

8. *O Paradiso!*   h. Kay Nolte Smith
9. *Murder at the Opera*   i. Conrad L. Osborne
10. *The Divas*

Extra Credit:

A. Author-illustrator Edward Gorey has published a macabre
tale about a diva stalked by a crazy fan. What is its title and
what is the diva's name?

B. A 1975 novel by James McCourt, which concerns a cult surrounding a mezzo, has become something of a cult classic in
and of itself. What is its title?

C. The story concerned the creation of a Wagnerian-like opera
called *The Giant*. The author was a famous mystery writer
breaking away from her genre work under the pseudonym of
Mary Westmacott. Give the title and author of the book.

71. IT'S A LIVING

Can you match each operatic character at left with his or her
trade?

1. Katherine *Madame Sans-*   a. glass-cutter
   Gêne   b. blacksmith
2. Guccio *Gianni Schicchi*   c. cook
3. Sellem *The Rake's*   d. laundress
   Progress   e. prompter
4. Irene Giroux *Postcard*   f. butler
   from Morocco   g. doctor
5. Rabonnier *La Rondine*   h. bootmaker
6. Paolino *Il Matrimonio*   i. dyer
   Segreto   j. hatmaker
7. Cal *Regina*   k. vicar
8. Mr. Gedge *Albert Herring*   l. painter
9. Assan *The Consul*   m. auctioneer
10. Euthycles *La Belle Hélène*   n. bookkeeper
11. Quince *A Midsummer*   o. carpenter
    Night's Dream

12. M. Javelinot *Dialogues des Carmélites*
13. Creonte *The Love for Three Oranges*
14. Frick *La Vie Parisienne*
15. M. Taupe *Capriccio*

Extra Credit:

A. In what opera does a photographer put forth that laborers want to be tradesmen; tradesmen, lords; lords, artists; and aritsts, gods?

B. In what Offenbach work does a character describe, in an aria, an interview he has had at an employment agency where he has gone to seek a housekeeper?

C. What opera cast includes two journalists, four Spanish dancers, a waiter, a butler, and a fireman?

72. THE MODERN AGE

While we tend to associate opera with period settings, we forget that our own time has its own distinctive images and objects that have made their way into musical works.

1. What electrical appliance is an important element of *La Voix Humaine, The Consul,* and *Trouble in Tahiti?*

2. In what Poulenc opera is there a reference to ration cards?

3. What opera concerns the efforts of steelworkers to form a union?

4. In Jonathan Miller's controversial "Little Italy" *Rigoletto* staging, what "accompanies" the Duke as he sings *"La donna è mobile"?*

5. In what opera does a woman singing a lullaby to her grandchild promise the baby, among other things, planes?

6. In what Britten opera is a buzz-saw mentioned?

7. What Prokofiev opera concerns a Soviet pilot?

8. In what opera does a soprano sing to music issuing from a tape recorder?

9. In what opera does a saint pose for a photograph?

10. What short Douglas Moore opera takes place on the set of a hospital-type TV soap opera—complete with commercial breaks?

Extra Credit:

A. In what opera is Einstein depicted?

B. In what operetta is a character called Microscope?

C. What is the name of the movie Dinah describes in *Trouble in Tahiti?*

73. STARS AND BARS

If you "love a military man," go to the opera! Can you identify the correct rank of these soldiers, sailors, and guards?

1. Rohnsdorff *Die Csárdásfürstin*
2. Don José, before his downfall
3. Belcore
4. Prince Gremin, upon his retirement
5. Silas Slick
6. Otello
7. Cassio
8. Narraboth
9. Rudolph *Guillaume Tell*
10. Junius *The Rape of Lucretia*
11. Mary *Die Soldaten*
12. Haudy *Die Soldaten*
13. Pirzel *Die Soldaten*
14. Mr. Redburn
15. Mr. Ratcliffe

Extra Credit:

A. In *Carmen Jones,* Oscar Hammerstein's libretto updates the Bizet score to 1943 America, opening at a Southern parachute factory. What famous black pilot puts in an appearance?

B. What is Marie's regiment?

C. In Hasse's *Cleofide,* Gandarte and Timagere are military enemies. With whose army is each a general?

74. MUCKY-MUCKS

Can you match each operatic character at left to his or her title?

1. Simon Boccanegra
2. Federica *Luisa Miller*
3. Don Julien *Don Rodrigo*
4. Hermannn *Tannhäuser*
5. Rodrigo *Don Carlos*
6. Don Pedro *La Périchole*
7. Don Magnifico *La Cenerentola*
8. Lucrezia Borgia
9. Charles Blount *Gloriana*
10. Robert le Diable
11. Ishmael *Nabucco*
12. Paul *La Grande-Duchesse de Gérolstein*
13. The Marschallin *Der Rosenkavalier*
14. Amfortas *Parsifal*
15. Dom Sébastien

a. Governor of Ceuta
b. Marquis of Posa
c. Duchess of Ferrara
d. Duchess of Ostheim
e. Duke of Normandy
f. Doge of Genoa
g. Prince of Stein-Stein-Steis-Laper-Bott-Moll-Schorstenburg
h. King of Portugal
i. Princess of Werdenberg
j. Governor of Lima
k. Lord Mountjoy
l. King of Monsalvat
m. Baron of Montefiascone
n. Landgrave of Thuringia
o. King of Jerusalem

Extra Credit:

A. What political appointment does Count Almaviva say he has received, in *Le Nozze di Figaro?*

B. In the definitive edition of *Candide,* five royal characters sing a barcarolle. What are their names?

C. In *Mignon,* Philine is invited to a celebration in whose honor?

75. THE BAKER'S DOZEN

In what operas are the following "menus" featured?

1. Hens, marinades, buns, pastry, candy, vanilla, coffee

2. Eggs, ham, mustard, cress, strawberry jam, muffins, toast, Sally Lunn, and a "rollicking" bun

3. A little venison, a superb pâté, a succulent pudding

4. Turkey, ham, gravy, french-fried potatoes, plum pudding, cheese, pie, nuts

5. Six pullets, three turkeys, two pheasants, one anchovy

6. Hors d'oeuvres, spices, fish, chicken, crayfish, duck pâté

7. Bacon, butter, flour, sausages, eggs, beans, onions, coffee

8. Chocolate layer cake, marzipan, carob, rice pudding, cream, raisins, almonds, figs

9. Spring onions, leeks, watercress, cabbages, sage, fowl, a ham, sausages, salted meats

10. Oil, hazelnuts, walnut bread, flour, cheese, lentils, eggs, butter, currants

11. Roasted stag, a turkey, lobster

12. Jelly, pink blancmange, iced seedy cake, treacle tart, sausage rolls, trifle, chicken, ham, cheese straws, marzipan

13. Cakes, jellies, custard, chocolate dates, fruit salad, trifle, cream-filled pastries, almond favors

Extra Credit:

A. In what opera does a chorus feasting on turkey ask who wants to be served the "pope's nose"?

B. In what opera does a family rhapsodize over an omelette?

C. In what opera is there a character called Tapioca?

76. A MUSICAL GAZETEER

The places at left do not necessarily become the settings of, yet are mentioned in, the works at right. Match them up.

1. The Pindus Mountains
2. Knightsbridge
3. South Kensington Station
4. Mount Etna
5. Tremorden Castle
6. Poland
7. Castiglion Prison
8. The Peronnet Bridge
9. Guadalquivir
10. Milan
11. Armenia
12. Borgognone
13. The South Pacific
14. La Musée d'Artillerie
15. Montauban

a. *The Mikado*
b. *The Pirates of Penzance*
c. *La Rondine*
d. *Andrea Chénier*
e. *Les Contes d'Hoffmann*
f. *La Vie Parisienne*
g. *Lulu*
h. *Iolanthe*
i. *The Sorcerer*
j. *Mosè in Egitto*
k. *Manon*
l. *Rigoletto*
m. *Fedora*
n. *Don Quichotte*

Extra Credit:

A. Ping, Pang, and Pong own property—respectively, a house on a lake, a garden, and forests. Where are they located?

B. Act IV of an Italian opera is titled "The Orfano Canal." Name the opera.

C. What operatic heroine snarls, *"Al diavolo l'America!"* ("To hell with America!")?

77. GIFT HORSES

Gifts abound in opera. How generously can you answer the following questions?

1. What does Harry give Minnie in *La Fanciulla del West?*

2. Who once owned—or so he says—the jewels that Horace Tabor gives Baby Doe as a wedding gift.

3. How many louis does Violetta tell Annina to give to the poor?

4. What did Prince Obolowsky give Baba the Turk?

5. What was Don Basilio once given to wear, to teach him a lesson, as he relates in *Le Nozze di Figaro?*

6. What does Elisabeth of Valois give to a woman who has lost her two sons in battle?

7. What character in a crossover work reminisces about her old love affairs, one of which netted her a "tiny Titian"?

8. In *Simon Boccanegra,* what area has the King of Tartaria opened to Genoan fishing vessels as a gesture of peace?

9. Who promises Bergdorf Goodman clothes to a girl he'd like to seduce?

10. What gift does Golaud promise Yniold for spying on Pelléas and Mélisande?

11. What did Mandryka once do to please a lady friend who had wanted to go sleigh-riding in July?

12. What is Andrew's anniversary gift to Abbie in *Lizzie Borden?*

13. Who buys Lodoletta red wooden shoes as a birthday gift?

14. What is Nellie's Christmas gift to Alma in *Summer and Smoke?*

15. What is the Prince's gift to Philine in *Mignon?*

Extra Credit:

A. Arabella has three suitors: Count Elemer, Dominick, and Lamoral. Name the gift each man brings her.

B. Who is offered, among other treasures, chrysolites, beryls, rubies, and chalcedony to divert her attention from another attraction?

C. Albert Herring is given three prizes for being King of the May. What are they?

78. THE PITS

Conductors are, of course, indispensible to opera performances. How knowledgeable are you about some of these leaders in the field?

1. Who was the first woman to conduct the Royal Opera at Covent Garden?

2. What French conductor made his Met debut at the age of seventy-four, leading a performance of *Samson et Dalila?*

3. What conductor, associated with the Philadelphia Orchestra and Teatro alla Scala, will not work with singers who interpolate high notes?

4. Which of the world's foremost conductors of Wagner did not make his Bayreuth conducting debut until the age of seventy?

5. Who was the first Englishman to conduct at the Bayreuth Festival?

6. What maestra founded the Opera Orchestra of New York?

7. What conductor, who has made over one hundred recordings, edited and recorded Rameau's unfinished *Les Boréades?*

8. At what opera house did Cal Stewart Kellogg make his professional debut?

9. What conductor began a seven-year "Viva Verdi" festival in 1994, presenting all twenty-eight of the composer's operas in order of composition, as free parks concerts?

10. Zubin Mehta made his U.S. conducting debut at the podium of what opera production?

11. What conductor, making his New York City Opera debut on 8/19/84, called for an unauthorized encore of one of the numbers in *La Rondine?*

12. What conductor composed an opera entitled *Lou Salomé?*

13. What American conductor became the music director of L'Opéra de Lyon in 1989?

14. What Moscow-born conductor was elected music director of the then-Soviet Kirov Opera in 1988, despite never having been a member of the Communist Party?

15. What Italian conductor became music director of the Welsh National Opera in 1992?

Extra Credit:

A. What American conductor was invited in 1982 to lead the Central Opera Company of Peking's *La Traviata*—on its home ground?

B. What experienced Janáček conductor coincidentally celebrated his sixty-fifth birthday on the podium of a Covent Garden performance of *Kátya Kabanová?*

C. When inclement weather prevented much of the Philadelphia Orchestra from arriving at the Academy of Music for their 2/11/94 all-Wagner concert, what conductor brought his own piano transcriptions and accompanied the stalwart singers himself, at the keyboard?

79. A MUSICAL BOUQUET

If they're lucky, opera singers receive floral tributes from adoring fans. The characters they play are also not unacquainted with plants and blossoms.

1. In what kind of grove is the first scene of *Mireille* set?

2. What flower does Cio-Cio-San place in her hair as she awaits Pinkerton's return?

3. What tree does Walther sing about as he demonstrates his Prize Song to Hans Sachs at Hans's workshop?

4. During *Street Scene,* Sam and Rose sing a song set to a Walt Whitman poem about what kind of plant?

5. What centerpiece does Erika order for the dinner table as *Vanessa* opens?

6. Adrianna Lecouvreur dies from inhaling the scent of poisoned flowers. What species of blossom are they?

7. What flowers does Lulu wear in the bodice of her evening gown in Act II Scene 1 of *Lulu?*

8. What flower does Lucretia send her husband after she's been raped, with the message that it's from a Roman harlot?

9. What flowers adorn the costume of the Queen of the Fairies in Verdi's *Falstaff?*

10. What poisonous plant does Lakmé nibble on?

11. In *Le Jongleur de Notre-Dame,* Boniface sings about a simple plant that opened to form a cradle for the infant Jesus. What plant was this?

12. In what kind of tree does Mélisande's hair become entangled?

13. What herbal essence does Kundry use to heal Amfortas's wound?

14. What kind of flowers does Suzel bring her friend Fritz on his birthday?

15. What flower does Walter sing about in *La Wally?*

Extra Credit:

A. What kind of wood was the magic flute carved from?

B. In what opera does adding an enamelled rose to her clothing allow one woman to pass as another?

C. Why does Sophie sniff at the Silver Rose?

80. PERSONAL REFERENCES

The following people are spoken of, but do not appear, in their respective operas. Can you name these characters?

1. Albert Herring's aunt.

2. The sage whose proverbs Suzuki quotes to Pinkerton.

3. William Jennings Bryan's political opponent in *The Ballad of Baby Doe.*

4. The adventuress who betrayed Ramerrez in *La Fanciulla del West.*

5. The first apprentice to die while in Peter Grimes's service.

6. The Biblical figure to whom Eva compares Walther when she sees him in church.

7. Cassio's girlfriend, in Verdi's *Otello.*

8. Ortrud's father.

9. Suor Angelica's younger sister.

10. The Irish rebel Elizabeth I hopes to overthrow, in *Gloriana.*

11. The religious figure to whom le Comte des Grieux sarcastically compares his son.

12. The name under which Madeleine de Coigny will die in *Andrea Chénier.*

13. The man for whom *Capriccio's* ballet dancer will perform the next day.

14. The woman Robert Storch is falsely accused of having an affair with, in *Intermezzo.*

15. The woman to whom Dr. Schön is engaged in *Lulu.*

Extra Credit:

A. With whom are Wilhelm, Hermann, and Nathanael in love, in *Les Contes d'Hoffmann?*

B. Who were Pagliaccio, Mezzetino, Cavicchino, Burattin, and `Pasquariello?

C. In what operetta are the names of Lord Nelson, Fielding, Queen Anne, Mr. Micawber, and Madame Tussaud—among others—linked in a song?

81. ACTION!

No matter how old an opera is, a director will always find something new to do with it, as the following have illustrated:

1. The Met is the second company for whom Franco Zeffirelli has staged *La Bohème.* Name the first.

2. With what opera company did Renata Scotto make her directorial debut in 1987?

3. What director has earned the nickname "the bad boy of opera," for his updated stagings that have included *Le Nozze di Figaro* set in Trump Tower and *Tannhäuser* drawing televangelistic parallels?

4. What production marked Luciano Pavarotti's directorial debut?

5. With what opera company did Jonathan Miller make his U.S. directorial debut?

6. Who directed the Met's 1992 "coffin" *Lucia di Lammermoor?*

7. Who both conducted and directed New York City Opera's 1976 televised *Il Barbiere di Siviglia?*

8. What was filmmaker Lina Wertmuller's first attempt at staging live opera?

9. What was Harold Prince's first Met production?

10. What soprano, called the "Callas of Soubrettes," turned to directing in the 1980s, for such companies as the San Francisco Opera and the Met?

11. What director's trademark was a palette of neutral colors (though his *Manon* dressed its heroine in fiery red)?

12. What opera did mezzo-soprano Regina Resnik stage in her directorial debut in 1971?

13. In 1993, who was the first black director to stage *Porgy and Bess* for a professional American opera house?

14. Who created a ninety-minute version of Bizet's opera, called *La Tragédie de Carmen?*

15. What Argentinian staging director was Artistic Director of the Cincinnati Opera in the early 1960s?

Extra Credit:

A. What opera staging director produced a documentary film entitled *Divas?*

B. What Iranian staging and opera company director was delivered stillborn but then revived, resulting in his being named "Kindness of God" in his native tongue?

C. Identical twin directors who almost always work on mutually exclusive projects have made a name for themselves for their innovative stagings of both rare works and standards. Who are they?

82. SONDHEIM

In the world of musical theater, there are "Sondheimites" and "Webberites." Though the latter's *Phamtom of the Opera* is a big hit, it is the former's works that are making their way into opera houses in a crossover move unusual for occurring during the composer-lyricist's own lifetime.

1. What was the first opera company to stage *Sweeney Todd* in 1984?

2. In *Sweeney Todd,* there is a joke about the difference between Italianate and Irish tenors. What operatic tenor created the role of Pirelli on Broadway?

3. What operatic baritone played *Sweeney Todd* in the work's debut on the opera stage?

4. What is Adolfo Pirelli's real name?

5. What film of a Sondheim work—released in 1978 and poorly reviewed—won an Academy Award for its Adaptation Score?

6. Who wrote the above adaptation, and is closely associated with Stephen Sondheim as orchestrator of many of his shows?

7. What conductor has led the majority of Stephen Sondheim's shows on Broadway, as well as New York City Opera performances of *Sweeney Todd* and *A Little Night Music?*

8. What is unusual about the score of *A Little Night Music,* as compared to other musical theater works of its era?

9. What composer/conductor is name-dropped in "The Ladies Who Lunch" in *Company?*

10. In "Remember?" from *A Little Night Music,* an opera is named as having been "belched" by a boatman during a romantic rendezvous. Name the opera.

11. What coloratura soprano sang the role of "Young Heidi" in the New York Philharmonic concert performance of *Follies* recorded in 1985?

12. Who sang the part of the mature Heidi at that same performance?

13. What British opera company produced and recorded *Pacific Overtures* in 1987?

14. On what recording can Stephen Sondheim be heard accompanying a singer's rendition of "Send in the Clowns"?

15. On what recording can one hear the composer himself singing one of his own compositions?

Extra Credit:

A. Name the five "Liebeslieder" characters in *A Little Night Music*.

B. What university faculty did Stephen Sondheim join in 1990, as its first Cameron Mackintosh Professor of Contemporary Theatre?

C. In Sondheim's *Passion*, the first sound we hear of one character is of him singing a snippet from *L'Elisir d'Amore*. Who is he?

83. NO PLACE LIKE HOME

Match the household objects at left to the opera in which they are named.

1. Wicker chair	a. *H.M.S. Pinafore*
2. Dustbin	b. *La Rondine*
3. [Laundry] basket	c. *La Bohème*
4. Band-Aids	d. *Albert Herring*
5. A nail	e. *La Gazza Ladra*
6. Ladder	f. *The Last Savage*
7. Screen	g. *Falstaff*
8. Gridiron	h. *Sweeney Todd*
9. Kitchen faucet	i. *L'Enfant et les Sortilèges*
10. Oriental rugs	j. *Vanessa*
11. Stair-railing	k. *Werther*
12. Wallpaper	l. *Der Freischütz*
13. Silver spoon	m. *Rigoletto*
14. Mirrors	n. *Street Scene*
15. Harpsichord	o. *La Pomme d'Api*

Extra Credit:

A. What operatic family gets dispossessed during *Street Scene?*

B. What operatic character says that she hasn't sat down in a room with curtains, a sofa, and pictures for two years?

C. Which opera opens with a command concerning the placement of a blue sofa?

84. MICRO AND MACRO

Science, from the splitting of the atom to the wonders of the universe, plays a part in a number of operas.

1. In what Haydn opera is a man, transported merely to another's garden, duped into thinking he has gone to the moon?

2. In whose opera is the moon stolen from the sky?

3. Who puts it back?

4. In what opera does Merlin control a space ship that can time travel?

5. In *Street Scene,* what is described as being three parts high octane and one part atom bomb?

6. In whose Spoleto Festival USA staging of *Madama Butterfly*—set in World War II Nagasaki—did a simulated atom bomb explosion conclude the opera?

7. Robert Ward composed an opera about the responsibilities of a nuclear physicist. Name the opera.

8. What is considered the world's first opera inspired by the modern space age?

9. What is the name of a Janáček opera in which a burgher, in a drunken stupor, travels back in time to the 1400s and also visits the moon?

10. For his seventieth birthday, what space-age opera did Gian Carlo Menotti compose?

11. What Offenbach operetta is based upon a Jules Verne story?

12. What Menotti opera concerns a schoolbus attacked by aliens?

13. What frightens the creatures away?

14. Who composed an operetta entitled *Frau Luna?*

15. In that work, how do the characters ascend to the moon?

Extra Credit:

A. What Gilbert and Sullivan character claims that he can trace his family back to "a protoplasmal primordial atomic globule"?

B. The universe-traversing *The Voyage* is set, in part, in 2092. Name its visionary librettist and designer.

C. In 1988, the same two people collaborated with its composer on another airborne work, set a little closer to home. What was it?

85. CONSECRATED PLACES

Can you match these religious structures to the operas they relate to?

1. The monastery of St. Just	a. *Lizzie Borden*
2. St. Sulpice	b. *La Forza del Destino*
3. The convent of the Madonna degli Angeli	c. *La Gioconda*
	d. *Manon*
4. The Cathedral of Toledo	e. *Tosca*
5. Old Harbor Church	f. *Lodoletta*
6. San Marco Basilica	g. *Don Carlos*
7. Nostra Donna d'Atocha	h. *Don Rodrigo*
8. Church of Sant' Andrea della Valle	i. *La Battaglia di Legnano*
	j. *I Lombardi*
9. Saint Ambrogio Church	
10. Saint Guido's	

Extra Credit:

A. What does the title character in *The Saint of Bleecker Street* take as her name when she becomes a nun?

B. With which monastery is Ferdinand associated in *La Favorite?*

C. What is the name of the congregation sponsoring the picnic in *Porgy and Bess?*

86. IN THE HABIT

Nuns, abbesses, monks, vicars, priests, not to mention the occasional anonymous mystical hermit...opera plots certainly don't lack for characters who "keep the faith." Can you match these fifteen, at left, to the works they appear in?

1. Suor Osmina		a.	*Albert Herring*
2. Rangoni		b.	*La Forza del Destino*
3. Rev. Horace Adams		c.	*Boris Godunov*
4. Albine		d.	*The Ballad of Baby Doe*
5. Mr. Gedge		e.	*Suor Angelica*
6. Padre Guardiano		f.	*Lizzie Borden*
7. Don Marco		g.	*Le Jongleur de Notre-Dame*
8. Mme. de Croissy		h.	*Thaïs*
9. Balthazar		i.	*Peter Grimes*
10. Father Chappelle		j.	*The Saint of Bleecker Street*
11. Rev. Harrington		k.	*Dialogues des Carmélites*
12. Boniface		l.	*Attila*
13. Rev. Salvation		m.	*The Cradle Will Rock*
14. Leone		n.	*The Sorcerer*
15. Dr. Daly		o.	*La Favorite*

Extra Credit:

A. In *Suor Angelica,* mention is made of the royal parents of the title character. What are their names?

B. Name the four Elders in *Susannah.*

C. What church rank does Pooh-Bah hold in addition to his many other titles?

87. NATIVE AMERICANS

In opera, Native Americans are often represented by now "politically incorrect" characters and plot treatments. Too, some of the best-known Central or South American composers wrote to please European audiences. With these circumstances in mind, consider the following:

1. *O Escravo* (a.k.a. *Lo Schiavo,* or The Slave) incorporates native Brazilian Indian music into its score. Who composed it?

2. *Il Guarany* was dedicated to what public figure?

3. In that opera, Indians sing about objects that are understandably distressful to their Portuguese invaders. What are the disturbing items?

4. In Félicien David's *La Perle du Brésil,* a Brazilian Indian maiden is selected as a souvenir by an elderly admiral. What is her name?

5. What European opera composer wrote a two-act ballet called *Les Mohicans?*

6. The 1768 opera called *Le Huron,* by another European composer, tells the story of a white child who is raised by Huron Indians and then introduced to French society. Who wrote the music?

7. Thea Musgrave's *Simón Bolívar* incorporates into its score an Incan hymn composed for the real Bolivar's arrival at Bogotá. In what language is it sung in the opera?

8. Victor Herbert wrote an opera in which an Indian girl becomes a nun at a Santa Barbara mission. What is the title of the work?

9. Reynaldo Hahn preferred to compose operas about locales other than his native Venezuela. Where was his first, *L'Ile de Rêve,* set?

10. Although he wrote three operas, Alberto Ginastera never set one in his native country. Where was he born?

11. In 1917, American composer Henry Hadley wrote a tragic opera about the religious clash between native Mexicans and Christians. (You can guess who won by the fact that the opera concludes with *"Gloria in Excelsis Deo."*) Name the opera.

12. What Brazilian composer, better known for other kinds of works, wrote nine operas including one entitled *Jesus?*

13. A Lortzing opera about Peru never made it to a premiere. What was its title?

14. The original production of a 1695 Purcell opera featured a singer wearing a genuine Aztec feather dress. Name the opera.

15. Who wrote the music for Act V of that opera?

Extra Credit:

Let's not forget that a large section of America exists *north* of the U.S. border!

A. What is considered the first Canadian opera?

B. What city is the home base of the Canadian Opera Company?

C. In 1899, the Met's first tour outside the United States made its first stop at what foreign city?

88. IT'S GREEK TO ME

The lines at left occur in works that are otherwise primarily sung in another language. These extracts range from French and Latin to Japanese and even Greek! Can you match them to to their operas?

1. *"Çok yaşa yavrum!*	a. *Capriccio*
2 *"Quod erat demonstratum"*	b. *I Vespri Siciliani*
	c. *La Forza del Destino*
3. *"Addio, mia vita, addio"*	d. *Sapho*
	e. *Owen Wingrave*
4. *"De profundis..."*	f. *Madama Butterfly*

5. *"Le chapeau Pamela"*
6. *"Tales Patris, talem Filias"*
7. *"Largo, largo! Pizzicato, pizzicato!"*
8. *"Sic itur ad astra"*
9. *"Wir wollen essen!"*
10. *"Polremus"*
11. *"O ni! bikkuri shakkuri to!"*
12. *"Buon' giorno, signorine!"*
13. *"O Kami! O Kami!"*
14. *"Evoe"*
15. *"La Gloire c'est tout"*

g. *Candide*
h. *The Mikado*
i. *Der Rosenkavalier*
j. *The Ghosts of Versailles*
k. *La Vie Parisienne*
l. *La Cenerentola*
m. *The Gondoliers*
n. *Orphée aux Enfers*

Extra Credit:

A. What 1992 opera boasts a character whose vocabulary consists solely of the word "Ech!"?

B. In what French opera is there a maharajah whose lines—including a lengthy aria—are always in doubletalk?

C. In what French opera does a string of Oriental nonsense phrases include the name "Sessue Hayakawa"?

89. BARGAIN BASEMENT

Opera plots sometimes include scenes with street vendors, or other instances of items being bought or sold.

1. In what opera are cakes, handkerchiefs, bananas, betel leaves, mats, honeycombs, and slippers sold at a marketplace?

2. In what opera are leeks, turnips, prunes, strawberries, cream cheese, cabbage, and green sauce hawked by vendors?

3. In what opera do open-air salespeople offer slippers, rouge, beauty spots, ruffles, kerchiefs, hoods, songs, lottery tickets, powder, tobacco graters, ribbons, cane, and hats?

4. In what opera do early-morning greengrocers sell carrots, watercress, peas, birdseed, and artichokes?

5. Who offers for sale barometers, hygrometers, thermometers...and eyes?

6. Whose shop specializes in "vegetables, flowers, and seasonal fruits"?

7. It's Christmas eve, but in what opera are the following still on sale for people who need to complete their holdiay shopping: orange trees, dates, hot chestnuts, trinkets, caramels, coconut milk, and sparrows?

8. In what opera does a woman buy devil-crabs from a vendor, and other people announce their merchandise as being honey and strawberries?

9. In what Weill work is a drugstore lauded for its selection of hot and cold food, including chicken hash, chop suey, and banana splits?

10. What Vaughan Williams opera includes sellers of shellfish, primroses, and ballads?

Extra Credit:

A. In what opera are the contents of a house put up for auction and, accidentally, the lady of the house as well?

B. In what Verdi opera do characters sell their jewelry *to* a peddler?

C. What twentieth-century one-act French opera concerns a man who tries to sell his wife, but even the devil sends her back as a bad bargain?

90. THE PEANUT GALLERY, PART I

"There is more of a Sublime in the snare-drum part of *La Gazza
Ladra* than in the whole of the *Ninth Symphony.*"
                              —Thomas Pynchon, *Gravity's Rainbow*

Below, comments that famous composers have made about others who have written operas. Can you identify the subject? For
extra credit, give the originator of the remarks.

1. "_____ is France's greatest composer, alas. A musician
   of great genius, a little talent."

2. "You were the beginnings of my life as an artist. I sprang
   from you. You are the cause and I am the consequence."

3. "_____ is sunshine."

4. "_____ has a sense of timing and punctuation which I
   have never been able to find a Richard Strauss."

5. "Something like a court composer to Kaiser Wilhelm II."

6. "_____'s music reminds me of a blissful, eternally
   youthful life before the Fall."

7. "He would do better to shovel snow instead of scribbling on
   music paper."

8. "_____ is obviously mad."

9. "He wrote marvelous operas, but dreadful music."

10. "Such an outstanding lack of talent was never before united
    to such pretentiousness."

11. "My cook understands more about counterpoint than he
    does."

12. "The Mozart of the Champs-Elysées."

13. "His music exasperates sometimes, but it never bores."

14. "Amazingly modern and, if one can say such a thing, near to
    me in spirit."

15. "He was the greatest composer that ever lived."

91. THE PEANUT GALLERY, PART II

"Direct *Salome* and *Elektra* as if they had been written by Mendelssohn. Elfin music."

—Richard Strauss

Which operas are discussed in the following quotes? For extra credit, identify the composers whose opinions are being expressed.

1. "I liked the opera very much. Everything but the music."

2. "It was painful from start to finish."

3. "A libretto that should never have been accepted on a subject that never should have been chosen [by] a man who should never have attempted it."

4. "The only perfect English opera ever written."

5. "Very commonplace, vulgar, and uninteresting."

6. "Truly, let us thank heaven that nothing worse can come after this."

7. "While listening to it all I thought of those lovely princesses in Sacher Masoch who lavished upon their young men most voluptuous kisses while drawing red-hot irons over their lovers' ribs."

8. "Marionette stage-music!"

9. "[Its composer] wrote the first and last acts of _____. God wrote the second."

10. "I heard _____ for the first time after the war and I confess I prefer Gilbert and Sullivan."

11. "How sublimely classical."

12. "It's organ grinder's stuff."

13. "I could not compose operas like _____ and _____. I hold them both in aversion."

14. "If that was music, I have never understood what music was."

15. "A sort of chromatic moan."

92. NOT NECESSARILY FOR YOUNG EARS

The operas at left are each based upon a children's story or fairy tale. Can you match each work to its composer at right?

1. *Higglety Pigglety Pop!*	a. Barab
2. *Little Red Riding Hood*	b. Glass
3. *Babar the Elephant*	c. Rossini
4. *The Emperor's New Clothes*	d. Knussen
	e. Stravinsky
5. *Cardillac*	f. Goldmark
6. *The Juniper Tree*	g. Bereznowsky
7. *Where the Wild Things Are*	h. Moore
	i. Hindemith
8. *The Cricket on the Hearth*	
9. *La Cenerentola*	
10. *Le Rossignol*	

Extra Credit:

A. What internationally famous diva starred in a TV series called "Who's Afraid of Opera"?

B. What were the names of her three puppet costars?

C. What children's book illustrator has designed productions of such operas as *The Love for Three Oranges* and *The Cunning Little Vixen?*

93. MET TRIVIA, PART I

How "up" are you on Met lore?

1. What was the first native-born American to perform a principal role at the Met?

2. Who was the founder of the Metropolitan Opera Guild?

3. What millionaire Met box-holder, after the work's U.S. premiere, demanded that *Salome* be destroyed because of its profanity?

4. What was the Met's first radio broadcast to feature Milton Cross?

5. What opera did New York's 11/9/65 blackout switch off from taking place?

6. With what production did Alfred Lunt make his Met debut as staging director in 1951?

7. On what date was the Met Centennial Gala?

8. What was the last season that the Met cancelled in its entirety?

9. Opening night at the Met's 1918-1919 season also marked the end of World War I: 11/11/18. What was the opera that night?

10. When was the first live radio broadcast from the Met?

11. In 1933, whose twenty-fifth year of association with the Met was celebrated with a gala performance in which every artist on the company roster appeared onstage?

12. What baritone, who joined the Met in 1926, delayed his retirement from singing in order to be able to perform during the final season at the old house—at the age of seventy-three?

13. What tenor was honored onstage when he broke the above singer's performance record, on 2/17/92, with his 2,396th appearance?

14. During the early 1930s, the Met season was not complete without a special performance in each season featuring company stars doing both serious numbers and specially-written comic skits. In 1935, one piece of the program was called "Nibelungen Ringling Brothers-Barnum Bailey & *Götterdämmerung.*" What was the name of this kind of Met event?

15. The Met has not been without nepotism. During one season, who silently portrayed the Queen of Shemakha onstage as coloratura soprano Maria Barrientos sang the role from the pit?

Extra Credit:

A. What three Met productions were staged by George Ballanchine?

B. What was the first opera by a U.S.-born composer to be performed on opening night of the Met's New York season in 1933—and what other opera had already been performed at that afternoon's matinee?

C. The Met's first season consisted of operas sung exclusively in one language, and its second season of operas sung only in another (in both cases, these included works performed in translation). Name the two languages.

94. MET TRIVIA, PART II

1. What was the first Handel opera to be performed by the Met, on 1/19/84?

2. James Levine celebrated his 25th anniversary at the Met the same season Met Titles were installed "over his dead body." What season did this occur?

3. What scheduled opera was cancelled in order to produce the Texaco 50th Anniversary Concert on 3/10/90?

4. Who is the first performer to be made a managing director of the Met?

5. On 12/11/52, what Met performance was broadcast live to movie theaters across the country?

6. What opera was dropped during the Met's 1941-1942 season, not to reappear until 1946, because of American sentiment regarding an event of World War II?

7. What is the latest season opening date in history of the Met?

8. Whose idea was the Mini-Met, the one-season program for developing artists?

9. What was the first opera to be televised live from the Met?

10. In what theater did the Met's first performance at Lincoln Center take place?

11. What singer made his U.S. recital debut on the Met stage in 1989?

12. During the 1952-1953 season, what opera was given at the Met in two versions, Italian and English?

13. What was the first opera performed in the Metropolitan Opera House at Lincoln Center?

14. What baritone made his Met debut during the 1985-1986 season as Falstaff, at the age of sixty-nine?

15. What Met-sponsored project, which lasted only two years, included an evening of modern pieces sung by Ella Fitzgerald, another night devoted to Latin American music, and another consisting of British works, among other programs?

Extra Credit:

A. Name the eight operas that the Met performed in May 1939 as their contribution to New York events relating to the World's Fair.

B. Which two Met performances were called off on account of the assassination of President Kennedy?

C. In 1954, the Met's opening night consisted of scenes from four Italian operas rather than of one complete, long work. Name the operatic selections.

95. ACROSS THE PLAZA

In New York operatic jargon, when one has just been speaking of the Met, "across the plaza" means New York City Opera (and vice versa)—a mock-genteel way of referring to these rivaling companies based at the same arts complex, Lincoln Center.

1. What was the first production of New York City Opera's national company (its touring division)?

2. During the fall 1952 and fall 1953 seasons, New York City Opera collaborated with what foreign company to produce a bilingual *Madama Butterfly?*

3. What New York City Opera "Summer Festival" never took place because its orchestra went on strike to protest having a summer season?

4. In 1991, New York City Opera presented a controversial updating of *La Traviata* that implied Violetta died of AIDS. Who directed it?

5. During New York City Opera's 1976 "Operathon" radio broadcast, the company performed excerpts from a bel canto work that has never otherwise been part of their repertory. Name it.

6. Who conducted the American premiere of *The Voice of Ariadne* at New York City Opera in 1977?

7. What opera was presented by the company in both English and Italian versions during its fall 1972 season?

8. What is the only New York City Opera production to date staged by Jerome Robbins?

9. What soprano made her company debut as Violetta in a performance that has been dubbed by opera fanatics as "the scream *Traviata*"—not because of the sounds coming from the stage, but as a result of the unexpected, bloodcurdling shriek let loose by a member of the audience at the beginning of Act II?

10. In what New York City Opera performance did Victoria de los Angeles make her only company appearance?

11. When did New York City Opera's warehouse fire, in which costumes for seventy-four productions were destroyed, take place?

12. In 1991, the company collaborated with Bill T. Jones/Arnie Zare & Co. on a black blues opera. What was it's name?

13. Arleen Augér's only appearances with the company were in 1969. What was her debut role with the troupe?

14. What West Coast opera company had a fifteen-year associa tion with New York City Opera during Beverly Sill's performing years?

15. On 11/7/81, an elderly attendee of a New York City Opera matinee fell to her death from the topmost tier of the theater. What opera had ended only moments before?

Extra Credit:

A. Name the seven New York City Opera general directors since the company's creation.

B. Name the three works and composers that comprised the company's 10/9/80 world premiere of "An American Trilogy."

C. In 1993, the company again presented a trio of staged premieres. Name the operas and their composers.

96. THE PRINTED PAGE

While newspapers and magazines are most commonly associated with opera with regard to reviews, there are also other connections between publications and the stage.

1. What operatic character is ordered by her father to read the newspaper aloud to him?

2. Who reads to the Marschallin from a scandal sheet?

3. In *Street Scene,* which character rails against the "capitalist press"?

4. In that same work, who sings a lullaby interspersed with a discussion of a tabloid article on the double murder that occurs during the opera?

5. What newspaper does Aschenbach buy in *Death in Venice?*

6. When the Painter in *Lulu* commits suicide, Lulu tells Dr. Schön that the news is worthy of putting out an extra edition of his paper. What headline does Dr. Schön propose?

7. In what opera is a newspaper ad for a farmhand read aloud?

8. What is the name of the newspaper vendor in *The Saint of Bleecker Street?*

9. What is the only way she expects to ever see her own picture in a paper?

10. In *La Grande-Duchesse de Gérolstein,* a gazette of what nationality is quoted from by Prince Paul?

11. What newspaper does Rodolfo lay as a tablecloth in *La Bohème?*

12. For what publication does he need to complete an article?

13. One of Rossini's rare failures concerns a Neapolitan man who places an ad in a Parisian newspaper in hopes of finding a husband for his daughter. Name the opera.

14. What New York opera critic sang minor tenor roles with New York City Opera from 1958 through 1960?

15. What composer, winner of a Grand Prix de Rome, wrote music criticism for the *Journal des Débats* and the *Gazette Musicale* in order to make ends meet?

Extra Credit:

Name all five newspapers represented by reporters in *Captain Jinks of the Horse Marines.*

97. AGE DISCRIMINATION

In opera, characters' ages are rarely crucial to the plot and yet, when supplied, they help fill out characters' personalities considerably.

1. In *Chérubin,* how old is the title character?

2. How old is Wowkle's baby?

3. In Massenet's *Manon,* how old is the title character in Act II?

4. In Puccini's *Manon Lescaut,* how old is the character said to be during Act II?

5. How old was Lulu when Dr. Schön met her?

6. What birthday does Frederic celebrate at the start of *The Pirates of Penzance?*

7. How old is Pirate Ruth?

8. How old is Antonia in *Les Contes d'Hoffmann?*

9. How old is Cio-Cio-San at the time of her marriage?

10. How old is Gianni Schicchi?

11. How old is Red Whiskers in *Billy Budd?*

12 How old is Magda Sorel in *The Consul?*

13. What age does the disguised Papagena tell Papageno that she is?

14. How old is the Grand Inquisitor in *Don Carlos?*

15. At what age does Iolanthe appear to have given birth to Strephon, by human calculation?

Extra Credit:

Match tnese characters to their ages:

A. Zita *Gianni Schicchi*	a. 55
B. Simone *Gianni Schicchi*	b. 22
C. Nella *Gianni Schicchi*	c. 60
D. Miss Wordsworth *Albert Herring*	d. 70
	e. 38
E. Albert *Albert Herring*	f. 26
F. Nancy *Albert Herring*	g. 49
G. Casanova *Casanova*	h. 45
H. Pascoe *The Wreckers*	i. 20
I. Pascoe's wife, Thirza	
J. Anna Reich *Die Lustigen Weiber von Windsor*	

98. FUN AND GAMES

Operatic characters have their hobbies too.

1. What sport does Sam play in the gym in *Trouble in Tahiti?*
2. In Act I of *Albert Herring*, why do the three children enter the greengrocer's?
3. At Flora's party in *La Traviata*, a song is sung about a toredor. How many bulls must he kill in one day in order for his sweetheart to accept his proposal?
4. In *Antony and Cleopatra*, who calls for a game of billiards?
5. What Berlioz opera contains a pantomimed hunting scene set in an African forest?
6. What verismo opera contains a song called the "Bicycle Aria"?
7. What opera ends with a choral salute to Olympic athletes?
8. At the start of Act II of *Le Roi de Lahore*, what game are the guards engaged in?
9. In what opera is there javelin and discus throwing?
10. What Offenbach work contains a word game that ultimately spells out "locomotive"?

Extra Credit:

A. What are the names of the child soloists who imitate Park Avenue types during *Street Scene's* "Street Games" ensemble?
B. In Leoncavallo's *La Bohème*, who deliberately loses at pool so that the money he pays up will cover the bohemians' dinner bill?
C. What American composer, generally only listed as having written two operas, also composed a chamber opera entiled *A Hand of Bridge?*

99. BREAK A LEG, PART I

Part of the excitement of attending live opera is being on the scene when the unexpected happens. Were you there for these performer mishaps, cancellations, and substitutions?

1. When family illness pulled Roberto Alagna out of San Francisco Opera's 9/22/93 *La Bohème,* what twenty-four-year-old tenor took over the role of Rodolfo?

2. What Irish mezzo made her Met debut on 10/18/84 in *La Clemenza di Tito*—not as the scheduled Annio, but substituting for Tatiana Troyanos in the role of Sesto?

3. By the time that the English National Opera had reached the last day of its 1984 U.S. tour, illness and fatigue had felled some of its performers. On this final day, 6/30/84, who sang Robert Devereux in the matinee performance of *Gloriana* and also performed the Duke of Mantua that evening?

4. On 1/7/69, the show at the Houston Grand Opera—a *Barbiere*—nearly didn't go on when its Bartolo, Andrew Foldi, succumbed to the flu and no cover was in the house. What bass volunteered to go on and performed the role with score in hand?

5. What Wagnerian soprano was sent off to the hospital by a falling (luckily, lightweight foam) beam during the 4/28/90 Met performance of *Götterdämmerung?*

6. What soprano—hired only as a cover for the season—made headlines for substituting for Anna Somowa-Sintow in *Simon Boccanegra* and for Montserrat Caballé in *Ernani* during her first Met season?

7. On 11/29/85, in a Connecticut State Opera performance of *The Consul,* what mezzo was pressed into singing both the Mother and the Secretary?

8. On 10/20/86, what Met Tosca suffered a jaw injury when her Scarpia, Juan Pons, became a little too energetic during Act II?

9. What soprano, attending the show merely as part of the audience, wound up singing Act II through the finale of *La Traviata* after Carol Vaness, in her debut in that role with the company, became too ill to finish singing Act I?

10. What soprano took over from the same place in 1987 after Gianna Rolandi, coincidentally also making her debut in that role with the company, sang only to the end of Act I?

11. Who rescued the San Francisco Opera's opening night *Otello* on 12/10/83—three and one-half hours after the curtain had been scheduled to go up—by flying in to replace the indisposed Carlo Cossutta?

12. What bass made his unscheduled New York City Opera debut as Giorgio Walton in 1981, because Justino Diaz, the second-cast artist who would otherwise be covering that role, needed to save his voice for *Nabucco,* also being performed by the company during that period?

13. On 10/20/85, Mirella Freni and Plácido Domingo both pulled out of the opening night production at the Houston Grand Opera and were replaced by Fiamma Izzo d'Amico and Giacomo Aragall. What was the opera?

14. What heldentenor cancelled his 1983 San Diego Opera *Lohengrin* engagement because he needed to have his tonsils removed?

15. Rockwell Blake sang only Act I of the 12/16/86 performance of the Met's *I Puritani,* then withdrew due to illness. Who took over the role of Arturo in Act III, in his company debut?

Extra Credit:

A. On 10/13/82, tenor Carlo Bini set off boos when he replaced Plácido Domingo in a Met *La Gioconda.* Though Bini braved out the evening, his conductor did not. Who conducted Acts I through III, and who then took over at the podium to finish the opera?

B. Which two tenors named Neil both called in sick for the 3/18/89 Met radio broadcast of *Werther*—and which *third* Neil went on in the title role?

C. The Met's 9/25/84 *Les Contes d'Hoffmann* had a unique turn-around: instead of starring one leading tenor and three leading ladies, it had one soprano as Hoffmann's loves—and three tenors as Hoffmann. Name the three "poets" who held the evening together.

100. BREAK A LEG, PART II

1. When Luciano Pavarotti could not get through the successive high C's in the 11/8/96 Met *La Fanciulla del West,* he finished the act but another tenor came on for Act II. Who?

2. Just before the interior of Rosina's home revolved into view during the Act I set change of the Met's 1/17/96 *Il Barbiere di Siviglia,* it came loose and noisily caved in. Once it was repaired, what soprano made her normal entrance but first crossed herself before singing *"Una voce poco fa"?*

3. At that same performance, what baritone who had made his house debut only five days earlier as Ping, sang Figaro on short notice when its scheduled singer canceled?

4. What singer sued Opera/Columbus after stage fog in a 1990 *Boris Godunov* caused an anaphylactic allergic reaction?

5. On opening night of New York City Opera's 1995-1996 season, William Stone felt under the weather and mimed the leading role of *Mathis der Maler,* another baritone singing his music from the orchestra pit. Who was the substitute vocalist?

6. When the San Francisco earthquake of 10/17/89 hit, what San Francisco Opera performance due to go on that night had to be called off?

7. In a live concert filmed for television, Cecilia Bartoli ably performed the florid *soprano* version of a Bellini aria when the mezzo score did not arrive in time. What was the aria?

8. What tenor suffered a serious heart attack during a dress rehearsal of *Siegfried* in Turin, but recovered in two years' time to not only sing but perform handstands in English National Opera's 1990 revival of *The Gambler?*

9. When the scheduled tenor could not appear at a 1989 Los Angeles performance, Plácido Domingo, who was slated to conduct that night, took over the role. What was it?

10. On 4/9/90 at Covent Garden, Reiner Goldberg was able to master no more than the first act of *Die Meistersinger.* What young heldentenor stepped in to perform Walther?

11. What soprano cancelled out of her first Normas in Seattle after injuring her back in an aerobic step class?

12. In the 1/17/92 *Tosca* produced by Opera Pacific, the eponymous diva dropped her knife and had to roundhouse Scarpia with her fist. Who was she?

13. What German opera house was destroyed by fire in 1987—set by an arsonist who believed it was an office building?

14. What opera house was destroyed by fire on 1/31/94?

15. What opera house was destroyed by fire on 1/29/96?

Extra Credit:

A. The 1/5/96 Met premiere of *The Makropoulos Affair* was halted within moments when the first person to sing collapsed onstage. Who was he?

B. What prophetic line proved to be his last words?

C. The curtain never even went up on the next scheduled performance of the same opera on the following Monday. Why?

101. CAT'S CHORUS

The premiere of *Il Barbiere di Siviglia* featured a performer not mentioned on the bill: a cat. It wandered onto the stage, and the already ill-behaved audience meowed along while the cast attempted to shoo it away. However, a number of other works fully expect kitties to be part of the show!

1. Douglas Moore created a children's opera with a feline, fairytale theme. What is its title?

2. What character in *H.M.S. Pinafore* shows how to swing a cat—"o'nine tails"?

3. In what opera does the line "*Tre volte miagola la gatta in fregola*" ("Three times, the tomcat has yowled his love-cry") occur?

4. What Italian composer of serious opera and keyboard pieces, a man knighted by King John V of Portugal no less, also wrote "The Cat's Fugue"?

5. What American composer of two operas also wrote a musical piece called "The Cat and the Mouse"?

6. What feline-named impresario was director of La Scala and the Met?

7. What Russian opera composer also created songs entitled "*Berceuses du Chat*" ("Lullabies of the Cat") and "The Owl and the Pussycat"?

8. What vocal register is needed to sing the female cat in *L'Enfant et les Sortilèges*?

9. What vocal register is needed to sing the male cat in the same work?

10. What is the name of the heroine of *The Last Savage?*

11. What famous contralto recorded a children's album entitled *Snoopycat?*

12. In *Paul Bunyan,* two cats sing a duet. What is its title?

13. In the musical *Cats,* which character sings a mock-operatic Italian number whose first line is "*In una trepida notte d'estate*"?

14. One of Jorge Martín's Saki-based quartet of short operas entitled *Beast and Superbeast* concerns a cat who displays, with pandemonious results, his proficiency with the human language. What is the name of the opera?

15. In the 1920s, President Calvin Coolidge made a present of his canary to a newspaperman's cat with whom the bird had forged an unusual friendship. What was the name of the bird?

Extra Credit:

And now, some equal time for dogs!

A. What is the name of the dog in *Paul Bunyan?*

B. To whose household does the dog in *The Cunning Little Vixen* belong?

C. In Judith Weir's *The Blond Eckbert,* Berthe becomes upset when Walther, all but a stranger to her, casually mentions the name of a dog she had known years before, a name even she had forgotten. What is it?

102. PITCH PIPES

1. What countertenor created the roles of Priest-Confessor in *Taverner* and Astron in *The Ice Break?*

2. What countertenor was the first to play Akhnaten?

3. What legendary countertenor portrayed Oberon in the world premiere of *A Midsummer Night's Dream?*

4. What other operatic role did he create?

5. He has recorded duets with his son, also a countertenor. What is the name of this high-pitched descendant?

6. Who played the first Military Governor in *A Night at the Chinese Opera?*

7. What countertenor portrayed an Asian activist in the world premiere of *Harvey Milk?*

8. In an unusual turn of casting, what countertenor sang the role of Baba the Turk in the Serviges Television film of *The Rake's Progress* produced in 1994?

9. What New York-based all-male troupe, which has performed internationally, sings standard female operatic roles in drag, at their proper pitch?

10. What is the name of their leading soprano?

11. Who is the first countertenor to win the Metropolitan Opera National Auditions?

12. What German countertenor made his Covent Garden debut in 1990 as Orlovsky?

13. What young countertenor rocketed to worldwide notice in 1995 for his performance in Glimmerglass Opera's *Tamerlano?*

14. What role had he performed with the Los Angeles Opera in 1993?

15. What countertenor shared the bill with him when he performed with Glimmerglass Opera in *L'Incoronazione di Poppea?*

Extra Credit:

A. For countertenors, 9/27/88 was a landmark date—the first time countertenors appeared in a Met production. What was the opera, and which two countertenors performed that night?

B. Gluck composed the roles of Orfeo and Orphée, for performance in Vienna and Paris, respectively, for two quite different kinds of voices. What were they?

C. The movie *Farinelli,* about a celebrated castrato, divides its title role among three artists. Who are they?

103. OPERA U.S.A.

In recent years, America's many opera companies have made important contributions to the art, especially with regard to new or neglected works, and in support of young American singers who no longer need to go to Europe to forge a career. How well do you know what's been happening around the country?

1. In 1992, the Manhattan School of Music presented the New York premiere of Ronald Perera's chamber opera based on a landmark feminist novella published one hundred years earlier. What was its title?

2. What opera had its U.S. staged premiere as late as 1995, in Arlington, Virginia—an event attended by the composer's own granddaughter, Simonetta Puccini?

3. What was the first opera ever presented, in that work's 1971 world premiere, in the Kennedy Center Opera House in Washington, D.C.?

4. What was the first U.S. opera company to perform all three of the composer's only complete operas in a special Monteverdi cycle in 1988?

5. What opera company gave Verdi's *Il Corsaro* its first complete U.S. staging in 1982?

6. What opera company presented, in 1994, the world premiere of Argento's *The Dream of Valentino,* based on the life of the legendary silent screen star?

7. What opera, which had its world premiere at the Houston Grand Opera in 1995, concerned the man considered American's first openly gay public official?

8. In 1995, what American opera company presented the U.S. premiere of the Naples (mezzo) version of *I Puritani?*

9. It was an American success story: In 1954, she joined the Lyric Opera of Chicago as a singer and typist. In 1981, she became the company's general director, stepping down during their 1996–1997 season due to ill health. Who was this woman?

10. With what company did P. D. Q. Bach's *The Abduction of Figaro* have its world premiere?

11. What zarzuela entered the company's repertoire during Plácido Domingo's 1996–1997 season as artistic director of the Washington Opera?

12. What opera company is believed to have produced the first U.S. staging of *Maskarade* in its original Danish, in 1995?

13. What work did the Utah Opera commission from composer David Carlson to commemorate Utah's hundredth year of statehood?

14. What tribe of Native Americans does it concern?

15. Known for their concert stagings of ambitious works, the Opera Orchestra of New York celebrated their silver anniversary in 1996. What was their first production, in 1971?

Extra Credit:

A. Two *different* operas based on *The Aspern Papers* coincidentally had their world premieres on the same date: 11/19/88. Where did the performances take place?

B. In their 1993–1994 season, New York's Dicapo Opera set a Donizetti opera in American-occupied, World War II–era Italy, some characters singing in English and others in Italian. What was the opera?

C. An imaginatively paired double bill of *Trouble in Tahiti* and *Cavalleria Rusticana* opened the 1995–1996 season of what American opera company?

104. GO FOR BAROQUE

It's never too late to appreciate early operas! Recent staged revivals and CD releases have made it easier than ever to answer such questions as:

1. William Christie's early music ensemble, Les Arts Florissants, is named for an opera by what composer?

2. The ensemble enjoys a close relationship with the Brooklyn Academy of Music. What was the first opera they performed there?

3. *"Ombra mai fu,"* known as Handel's "Largo," comes from what opera?

4. Purcell's *The Fairy Queen* eliminates, from its Shakespearean story line, the marriage of Hippolyta and Theseus, omitting the bride altogether. What character does Theseus become?

5. In what Rameau opera does Theseus travel to Hades to rescue a friend from Pluto's clutches?

6. What French conductor, born in 1962, has become one of the world's foremost champions of early opera?

7. Eighteenth-century French composer Jean-Joseph Cassanéa de Mondonville wrote an opera which opens with Prometheus granting life to all the statues in his palace. Name it.

8. In 1994, the Manhattan School of Music launched "The Handel Project," whose agenda is to produce one or two Handel operas per year. Who was its inaugural director?

9. What was the first opera produced by that project?

10. Himself a singer, dancer, and violinist, Lully created an eclectic range of theatrical works. Which is considered his first true opera?

11. What Italian composer was commissioned in 1660 to write an opera for the wedding of Louis XIV?

12. The earliest version of Monteverdi's *La Favola d'Orfeo,* produced in 1607, did not end happily. What happened to its title character?

13. The works and life of a French playwright have been used in over fifty operas. He also wrote libretti for his own contemporary, Rameau. Name the dramatist.

14. One of the most popular eighteenth-century librettos by Metastasio was set over fifty times, by composers ranging from Anfossi to Zingarelli. What was it?

15. In 1994, the Munich National Theater presented an updated *Giulio Cesare* that required the title character to wear a kilt, a bald wig, and Doc Martens. Who gamely performed the role so garbed?

Extra Credit:

A. Two seventeenth-century French brothers each wrote a different script for *Médée,* half a century apart. Name the siblings.

B. Whose libretto was used for, respectively, Cherubini's *Médée* and Marc-Antoine Charpentier's *Médée?*

C. Match each talented Scarlatti sibling to his or her chief profession:

I.	Alessandro	a.	singer
II.	Anna Maria	b.	composer
III.	Melchiorra	c.	violinist
IV.	Tommaso		
V.	Francesco		

105. WEDDING BELLS

How many of these operatic nuptials have you attended?

1. What famous operatic couple improvise their own private marriage ceremony in the open air, claiming, "*Tempio ed ara e un core amante*"—"A loving heart is both church and altar"?

2. What comic opera includes an "et cetera"-filled dictation of the marriage contract to a notary who keeps finishing the bridegroom's sentences for him?

3. Who witnesses Anatol's proposal to Erika?

4. In *Werther,* who is said to have been married for fifty years?

5. In that same opera, for how long have Bruhlmann and Katchen been engaged?

6. Why was Iolanthe banished from fairyland for twenty-five years?

7. Whose wedding opens Act II of *The Saint of Bleecker Street?*

8. How do Marco and Giuseppe choose their brides?

9. What gift does Elvino give Amina at their betrothal ceremony?

10. When is their marriage to take place?

11. What happens when the wedding bells in *Les Vêpres Siciliennes* ring to signify the wedding of Hélèna and Henri?

12. What grisly discovery is made during Katarina and Sergei's wedding reception in *Lady Macbeth of Mtsensk?*

13. What terrible thing happens during the wedding celebration of Antonida and Sobinen?

14. Where does the wedding reception for Baby Doe and Horace Tabor take place?

15. *Casanova,* composed by Dominick Argento, ends with the title character toasting a young pair of newlyweds. Who is the bride?

Extra Credit:

A. What three items does Elvira list as her nuptial adornments?

B. In *Iolanthe,* the Fairy Queen refers to what kind of marriage that had been prohibited in England at that time?

C. What well-known operetta librettist penned a play called *Engaged, or Cheviot's Choice?*

106. DEVILISH DOINGS

Twisted bargains and supernatural string-pullings are a specialty of opera's assorted demons.

1. In Gounod's *Faust,* where does Walpurgis Night take place?
2. In what country does Berlioz's *La Damnation de Faust* open?
3. In the Berlioz work, in what tavern do the students sing a drinking song?
4. In Boito's *Mefistofele,* what classical beauty does Faust meet?
5. With what sound does Mefistofele taunt God?
6. Where is Doktor Faust when he hears about the death of his lover?
7. Who becomes the bedeviled Tom Rakewell's wife in *The Rake's Progress?*
8. Tom Rakewell is insane in Bedlam by the end of the opera. In the final scene, who does he imagine himself to be?
9. What works of art inspired this opera?
10. What is the Devil's name in *The Devil and Kate?*
11. In what city does Ruprecht meet Faust and Mephistopheles?
12. Who does Webster defend in *The Devil and Daniel Webster?*
13. What is the religious order of the possessed nuns in *The Devils of Loudun?*
14. In *La Damnation de Faust,* which character sings the "Song of the Rat"?
15. In Gounod's *Faust,* who begins a "Song of the Rat" only to be interrupted?

Extra Credit:

A. Name the five Spirit Voices in *Doktor Faust.*
B. What is the name of the devil in Smetana's *The Devil's Wall?*
C. In what feminist opera does a character sing, "There is a devil creeps into men when their hands are strengthened"?

107. THE NEW WORLD

Fourteen ninety-two was not a record year for opera—an art form not to evolve for yet another century—but certainly numerous operas have early world explorers to thank for their existence.

1. In what language was the premiere of Milhaud's *Christophe Colomb* performed?

2. Milhaud's *Maximilien* is based on the life of what Central American ruler?

3. What is the title of the third opera to comprise Milhaud's New World trilogy?

4. Meyerbeer's *L'Africaine* concerns which real-life explorer?

5. What Turin-born composer produced an opera called *Cristoforo Colombo* in 1892?

6. What opera company gave this work its first U.S. staging a hundred years later?

7. Napoleon admired which Spontini work about the conquest of Mexico?

8. For Opera Rara, Patric Schmid created *Christopher Columbus,* whose score is patched from twenty-two operettas by a well-known French composer. Name the composer.

9. Where does Act IV of that work take place?

10. Whom does Columbus marry, according to Schmid?

11. What miraculous elixir does he discover in the New World?

12. What Philip Glass opera was commissioned by the Met to celebrate the quincentennial of Columbus's 1492 voyage?

13. During his first voyage, Columbus discovered Santo Domingo. What famous bel canto composer wrote an opera entitled *Il Furioso nell'Isola di San Domingo?*

14. On his second voyage to America, Columbus discovered Guadalupe. What Offenbach operetta concerns a pretty native of that locale?

15. What French opera-ballet dating back to the 1730s includes an act called "*Les Incas de Péru*" and another, "*Les Sauvages,*" about Native Americans?

Extra Credit:

A. In her 1949 Buenos Aires debut, Maria Callas sang a role she was never to perform again onstage. What was it?

B. What Italian conductor made his debut in Rio de Janeiro, substituting on short notice to conduct *Aida* from memory?

C. In the definitive Bernstein version of *Candide,* the "New World" that Candide visits is Peru, where he encounters an unscrupulous Governor. What is the Governor's name?

108. LITERARY BORROWINGS

It is interesting to note how many operas are based upon works of poets, novelists, and playwrights of a nationality other than their composers. For instance:

1. What American composer wrote an opera entitled *Lord Byron?*

2. What Shaw play is based upon the same theme as that of *Don Giovanni?*

3. What Shaw play is the basis for *Der Tapfere Soldat* ("The Chocolate Soldier")?

4. Puccini's *Le Villi* is based on a work by what German writer?

5. What Mascagni opera was inspired by another of that writer's works?

6. What Thomas opera is based upon a work by Goethe?

7. *Maometto II, Semiramide,* and *Tancredi* were all based on works by what French writer-philosopher?

8. Michael Balfe's *The Bohemian Girl* was inspired by the work of what Spanish writer?

9. Donizetti's *Maria Stuarda* traces back to what German writer?

10. Susa's *Dangerous Liaisons* is based upon an epistolary novel by what French writer?

11. Francesco Cilea's *L'Arlesiana* is based on a work by what French writer?

12. What opera by a Russian composer was based on an Italian comedy and premiered in Chicago in French?

13. *Die Schweigsame Frau* was inspired by a work by what English poet-playwright?

14. *Die Englische Katz* is based on a novel by what Frenchman?

15. That same composer also based an opera on the French novel *Manon Lescaut.* Name the opera.

Extra Credit:

A. Name two Verdi operas based upon works of Byron.

B. What two Donizetti operas are based upon other works of Byron?

C. What French writer not only provided a text for a Stravinsky opera-oratorio, but sometimes performed in it? Name the work as well.

109. TOTALLY MOZART

Opera's "bad boy" composer sure wrote a lot of good music!

1. About which opera did Emperor Joseph II remark, "Too many notes, my dear Mozart!"?

2. With what work did Mozart's *Der Schauspieldirektor* originally share the bill?

3. Mozart performed for Marie Antoinette when she was seven years old. In what city?

4. Which Mozart opera besides *Die Entführung aus dem Serail* takes place in a harem and contains a character called Osmin?

5. In what Mozart opera do the sons of the title character both fall in love with his third wife?

6. What pope awarded Mozart the Order of the Golden Spur?

7. What Mozart work concerns Alexander the Great?

8. In what Mozart opera does a countess join the household staff of a mayor?

9. Which Mozart opera is based on a parody of an opera by Rousseau?

10. What famous composer was Mozart's rival Salieri's special patron?

11. In Rimsky-Korsakov's *Mozart and Salieri,* what vocal register is assigned to the role of Mozart?

12. What was the first Mozart role written for a castrato?

13. Lorenzo da Ponte himself attended the American premiere of a Mozart work that he had coauthored. Which one?

14. What was the first Mozart work to be performed in London?

15. In honor of the two-hundredth anniversary of Mozart's death, Welsh-born writer-critic Paul Griffiths created a full-length opera incorporating twenty-four numbers from Mozart's own works. What is the title of the pastiche?

Extra Credit:

A. Mozart's father was an authority on what instrument?

B. Mozart's son Franz composed sonatas and concerti for what instrument?

C. Mozart's sister was a gifted keyboard player. Name her.

110. RAPID TRANSIT

Though notorious for standing stock-still by the footlights, in truth some opera characters really get around!

1. From what port is Manon to be deported?

2. What character in *Il Viaggio a Reims* details the contents of everyone's luggage?

3. What American-born composer wrote an opera called *Transatlantic?*

4. In what twentieth-century opera is the hero sent on his way to a lilting ensemble, "Bon Voyage"?

5. What 1991 opera is loosely based upon the travel writings of Alexandra David-Neel?

6. In what 1989 opera are scenes set in Somewhere, Nowhere, Today, and Tomorrow?

7. In *La Belle Hélène,* Menelaus is sent away to allow the romance of Helen and Paris to flourish. Where is he sent?

8. Gregori stops at an inn, in Act I, Scene 2 of *Boris Godunov.* To what country is he en route?

9. In *Dido and Aeneas,* Aeneas' boat is rocked by a storm as it heads for what country?

10. What piece of land does the Dutchman vow to sail around?

11. By what mode of transport does Robert leave Christine in Act I of *Intermezzo?*

12. In what opera does Act II begin with an innkeeper telling angry travelers that all the rooms have been taken?

13. In what Tippett opera do characters riot in an airport?

14. What Gilbert and Sullivan character would like to punish people who scrawl graffiti on train windows?

15. What city does Aschenbach leave for Venice?

Extra Credit:

A. In *The Good Soldier Schweik,* what train does Schweik ride?

B. Name the bus driver in *Help, Help, the Globolinks!*

C. In *Iolanthe,* what two Underground stations does the Lord Chancellor sing that he dreamt of, in his Nightmare Song?

111. THE NON-OPERA STAGE

Serious plays and musical comedies sometimes turn to opera for their inspiration.

1. *Master Class* is based on a series of master classes Maria Callas gave at Juilliard in 1971. Name its playwright.

2. Who created the role of Callas in its Broadway premiere?

3. The play shows the diva instructing just a handful of singers. How many students had signed up for the real Callas course?

4. The same playwright as the above wrote another play about Callas's recordings. What is its name?

5. That title refers to a pirated performance. When did it take place?

6. *Miss Saigon* updates the story of *Madama Butterfly* to the Vietnam War. Name the composer-lyricist team.

7. It took a petition of its members to keep Actors Equity from barring one member of the British production from being in the Broadway cast of *Miss Saigon*. Who was he?

8. A 1996 Pulitzer-finalist play by Jon Marans concerns an Austrian vocal coach who insists on teaching a young pianist to sing Schumann. Name the play.

9. The Pulitzer Prize for drama that year was awarded to a musical based on *La Bohème*. What is its title?

10. Who wrote its score, lyrics, and book?

11. What then-twenty-five-year-old wrote the original lyrics for Andrew Lloyd Webber's *Phantom of the Opera?*

12. What is the name of the opera divo in that work?

13. At what opera house does the action take place?

14. In 1988, *M. Butterfly* became the first Asian-American play to win a Tony. Who wrote it?

15. In 1993, *The Most Happy Fella* was revived on Broadway. What opera singer played the title role?

Extra Credit:

In Andrew Lloyd Webber's *Phantom of the Opera,* three different operas are shown in rehearsal or performance. What are their titles and composers?

112. MERMAIDS

Melodious sirens of the sea can be found in folk legends from around the world, and operas have answered their call. Can you answer these questions?

1. What novelist wrote the work that inspired both Lortzing and E. T. A. Hoffmann to write operas entitled *Undine?*
2. Name the knight that falls in love with Undine.
3. What American composer wrote yet another opera based on that novel, which had its world premiere by New York's Center for Contemporary Opera in 1995?
4. What Czech composer wrote *Rusalka,* an opera that is partially based on Hans Christian Andersen's "Little Mermaid"?
5. In this opera, which characters bear a distinct resemblance to Wagner's Rhinemaidens?
6. What is the name of the opera's resident witch?
7. What Russian composer wrote an opera called *Rusalka?*
8. On whose writings, however, did he base his work?
9. In the Russian *Rusalka,* the heroine was once a miller's daughter, who became a mermaid after being abandoned by a prince. What was her human name?
10. What is the name of the sea princess with whom Sadko falls in love?
11. What body of water forms the estate of her family's palace?
12. In what Italian opera does an orphan pledge herself to the King of the Rhine when spurned by the man she loves?

13. What Offenbach opera about mermaids had its premiere in Vienna, with a German libretto?

14. Sea females have a fondness for traveling in trios. In Act II of a Handel opera, the title character encounters three mermaids. Who is he?

15. What author of a mermaid tale, referred to in the above questions, himself wrote the libretto for an opera about water sprites?

Extra Credit:

A. In the year of his death, what German composer began an opera called *Loreley* but never completed it?

B. What Russian opera, based on the work mentioned in question 1, was completed but has never been performed?

C. In what opera do sirens invite humans to bathe with them, with the following entreaty: "Come, come, naked in for we are so. / What danger from a naked foe?".

113. KNOWING THE SCORE

It has become popular for orchestras to give screenings of movies, providing live accompaniment of their classical scores. Every opera composer on the left has written music for at least one film. Can you match each man to his respective movie?

1. Thomson	a. *Mayerling*
2. Weill	b. *New Babylon*
3. Bernstein	c. *Alexander Nevsky*
4. Korngold	d. *Hamlet*
5. Copland	e. *On the Town*
6. Shostakovich	f. *Lady in the Dark*
7. Walton	g. *Louisiana Story*
8. Gershwin	h. *Our Town*
9. Prokofiev	i. *Captain Blood*
10. Honegger	j. *An American in Paris*

11. Rota
12. Vaughan Williams
13. Glass
14. Thomson
15. Herrmann

k. *The 49th Parallel*
l. *Citizen Kane*
m. *La Dolce Vita*
n. *Koyaanisqasti*
o. *The Plow That Broke the Plains*

Extra Credit:

A. What Korngold-scored film included an original one-act opera?

B. The same directorial team that filmed *The Red Shoes* created a movie version of *Die Fledermaus*. What was it called?

C. What 1943 film saw the collaboration of Weill (lyrics), Copland (music), and Lillian Hellman (script)?

114. THICK AS THIEVES

Opera certainly has its share of crooks. In your listening, have you apprehended these?

1. In what Weill opera does a policeman shoot but then befriend a thief?

2. What American composer wrote an opera called *The Robbers,* based on a Chaucer tale?

3. A celebrated nineteenth-century bandit accused of 243 murders (he only admitted to 135!) is the subject of a Millöcker opera named for him. What is it?

4. A Schiller play about an eighteenth-century outlaw proved inspirational to Verdi. What opera did he base upon it?

5. Offenbach used the framework of a bandit comedy to mock the empire of Napoleon III. What is the title of this operetta?

6. In *Lakmé,* whose watch is stolen at the marketplace?

7. When Dick Johnson is caught in Act III of *La Fanciulla del West,* who turns him in?

8. In Ethyl Smyth's *The Boatswain's Mate,* a man pretends to rob an inn. Why?

9. Fra Diavolo passes himself off as what nobleman?

10. In *I Gioielli della Madonna,* who boasts that he would steal precious religious articles to prove his love for Maliella?

11. Who is the real thief?

12. In *The Old Maid and the Thief,* Miss Todd and Laetitia break into a store. What are they after?

13. In that same work, whose idea is it to steal a car?

14. In Act I of *Manon,* the title character and Des Grieux steal a carriage. Whose is it?

15. The year 1991 saw the world premiere of *The Death of Klinghoffer,* based on the hijacking of the cruise ship *Achille Lauro.* Who composed it?

Extra Credit:

Ethyl Smyth's opera *The Wreckers* is about Cornish villagers who turn off the lamp of their lighthouse to lure boats to crash, so they can loot the vessels. In what language was this opera originally written, in what language did it have its 1906 world premiere, and in what language was its premiere recording made in 1994?

115. NUDE SCENES

Opera-lovers sometimes get an eye- as well as an earful when they attend a show.

1. The Met's production of what Russian opera treated the audience to a male shower scene?

2. The woman who played the leading role of the above staging had made headlines when she herself appeared in the buff in *Salome.* Name her.

3. The Salomé in what Massenet work keeps her clothes on?

4. However, the pagan courtesan for which another Massenet opera is named has known to be performed, in part, in the nude. Who is she?

5. What opera, composed by Jay Reise and staged by Frank Corsaro for its world premiere at New York City Opera in 1988, included frontal nudity of both male and female actors?

6. In the taped-for-television premiere staging of *The Dangerous Liaisons,* the leading baritone, apparently wearing only a large shirt, simulated sex with female prostitute. Who was he?

7. The 1/95 *Opera* magazine cover was dominated by a full-color performance photo of Willard White clad only in a loincloth. What was the opera?

8. In what Massenet opera is a provincial young man shocked to learn that the woman he loves has posed nude for leading Parisian artists?

9. In what opera is an offstage bather ogled by her male neighbors?

10. In *Akhnaten,* the title character is momentarily undressed. Why?

11. Why does his body look so odd?

12. What Mascagni opera is about Lady Godiva?

13. Les Arts Florissants's staging of *Orlando* includes a nude actor occasionally doubling for one of the clothed singers as what character?

14. Rhoda Levine's 1991 New York City Opera production of what modern German opera included several nude rape victims?

15. A very short opera, *The Emperor's New Clothes,* was performed by the New York Philharmonic in 1949. Who composed it?

Extra Credit:

A. In *Kinkakuji*, which had its premiere in Berlin in 1976, a female character bares her breast and then invites a man to drink her milk from a cup. In what setting does this indeed kinky act occur?

B. The 1991 Royal Opera production of *Les Huguenots* turned the usually staid British audience into frothing hecklers during its chorus of bathers. Why?

C. In what modern opera does a courtesan recommend, in the most graphic language imaginable (yes, the "F-word," if you'll pardon our French!), that for the greatest sexual satisfaction, one should employ a Frenchman?

116. LOOSE ENDS

How much richer the opera repertoire would be had some composers finished what they had started!

1. Marc Blitzstein died before being able to complete an opera commissioned by the Ford Foundation. What was its title?

2. What composer put the finishing touches on *The Stone Guest, Khovanshchina,* and *Prince Igor?*

3. Though Schoenberg wrote the text for the third act of an opera, he never completed the music for it. The work is produced, through Act II, regardless. What is its title?

4. As noted in quiz 30, Halévy had several famous pupils. Which one finished his opera *Noë?*

5. *Les Vêpres Siciliennes* was created from a reworked libretto for what unfinished Donizetti opera?

6. Who completed *Doktor Faust,* left incomplete at the composer's death?

7. Chabrier was able to complete only one act of his last opera. What was its title?

8. Sir Edward Elgar started work on an opera, but didn't complete it. What was its literary inspiration?

9. What Sullivan operetta was left unfinished at his death and completed by Sir Edward German?

10. One of Kálmán's operettas had its premiere the year after his death, once it was completed by his son, Charles. Name it.

11. What composer commissioned Gertrude Stein to write the libretto for *Dr. Faustus Lights the Lights,* but then never wrote the music for it?

12. Respighi died before writing the last twenty-nine pages of *Lucrezia.* Who finished them?

13. In 1872, Cui, Mussorgsky, Rimsky-Korsakov, and Borodin were commissioned to write an opera-ballet together. When his colleagues abandoned the project, Rimsky-Korsakov finished the job. Name the opera.

14. Only fragments exist of an unfinished comic opera by Mozart, begun in 1783. What is it?

15. *Il Trovatore* is notorious for having one of the most confusing plots in all of opera. Possibly part of its problem may stem from its librettist, Salvatore Cammarano, having died before completing his revisions. Who finished the job for him?

Extra Credit:

A. What fragmentary Debussy opera was reconstructed and performed as a complete work by L'Opéra de Lyon to mark the 1993 opening of their new house, the Opéra Nouvelle?

B. Five of a composer's students—including d'Indy and Chausson—finished their mentor's opera, *Ghisèle,* following his death. Name the composer.

C. In 1978, William Bolcom completed and orchestrated Milhaud's unfinished 1937 arrangement of an eighteenth-century opera. Name the work.

117. ORIENTALISM

The East has provided exotic inspiration for many operas.

1. In *The Mikado,* when Ko-Ko announces he's found a volunteer wishing to be beheaded, how does the chorus respond?

2. In what country is *Turandot* set?

3. In what country is *Das Land des Lachëlns* set?

4. In what country is *Iris* set?

5. In what city does *Madama Butterfly* take place?

6. What year was Western opera first performed in Japan?

7. In what country is *Les Pêcheurs de Perles* set?

8. Though rarely made up or costumed to appear as such, Tamino is a prince of an Asian country. What is it?

9. Who composed *Ba-ta-clan?*

10. Who composed *Fisch-Ton-Can?*

11. On the heels of *The Mikado* came an operetta called *The Geisha,* which very much resembles *Madama Butterfly* in plot. Who composed it?

12. What French composer wrote an opera in 1893 on a similar theme?

13. Who composed *Nixon in China?*

14. Who composed *A Night at the Chinese Opera?*

15. In *Le Rossignol,* a mechanical bird is a gift from an Asian emperor. What could be said of the gizmo's nationality?

Extra Credit:

A. In 1992, the Washington Opera presented the American stage premiere of an opera by Jin Xiang. What was its title?

B. What was unusual about the design team of the *Madama Butterfly* produced in San Francisco by L'Opéra de Lyon in their first visit to that city?

C. What black baritone played the leading role of Mizoguchi in the 1995 New York City Opera premiere of Mayuzumi's *Kinkakuji?*

118. MAKING UP IS HARD TO DO

Opera characters are really very human, with "bad hair days" just like the rest of us. Were you there while these folk primped or complained?

1. What Gilbert and Sullivan character rages, "The maiden has bright brown hair / And mine is as white as snow"?

2. What Gilbert and Sullivan character offers, "If you like, I will cut my hair"?

3. What Gilbert and Sullivan character worries that she must soon prepare, "reduced, with rouge lip-salve, and pearly-grey," to "make up" for lost time?

4. About whom is "Paint the pretty face / Dye the coral lip" sung?

5. Who is made up and bewigged as the following is sung: "Tint with powder, touch with tincture / Lightly bind a willful curl"?

6. Who declares, "Let hair-pins lose their virtue"?

7. What cosmetic does Cio-Cio-San throw away when she senses Pinkerton does not approve of it?

8. What object does the Ragpicker in *Il Tabarro* offer Georgetta as the best find he's had all day?

9. What male operatic character imperiously calls for his "*Perükke*"—his wig?

10. Who tells Andrea Chénier to imagine the woman he awaits to have "*Il nero alla aiglia*"—"kohl-rimmed eyes"?

11. In *Ariadne auf Naxos,* the Tenor's first appearance requires what coiffeur?

12. Who mourns that he must, literally, flour his face to make it white?

13. Who sings, "Many a man's been caught for good / Caught for good in a woman's hair," as she combs and braids hers?

14. Who asks, "Wouldn't you like to have two maids / Scrubbing your shoulder blades / in a bubble bath's sweet perfume"?

15. Who complains, *"Mon coiffeur m'a ce soir indignement coiffée"?*

Extra Credit:

A. In *The Mikado,* what crimes might ideally result in their perpetrator being painted with walnut juice?

B. In *Death in Venice,* what three changes does the Barber make to Aschenbach's appearance in Scene 15?

C. In *The Midsummer Marriage,* Bella describes three cosmetic procedures. What are they?

119. TINTINNABULATIONS

Bells feature in a number of operatic works. Do these questions ring any for you?

1. Name the composer of *Il Campanello di Notte* ("The Night Bell").

2. Who composed *La Campana Sommersa* ("The Submerged Bell")?

3. Arias are usually named after their first lines. What is the alternative title for the famous "Bell Song"?

4. Who composed it?

5. Who composed the opera *Les Cloches de Corneville,* also known as "The Chimes of Normandie"?

6. Which character sings that work's "Song of the Bells"?

7. What bell-related legend is central to that opera's plot?

8. In *Gloriana,* a City Crier comes through proclaiming Roberto Devereux a traitor. Who else, does he warn, might be guilty of treason?

9. In what opera does a chorus make its exit while singing, "*Din, don—suona vespero*"—"Ding dong, rings the vesper bell"?

10. Hauptmann's *Die Versunkene Glocke* ("The Sunken Bell") was, in part, responsible for what Dvořák opera?

11. What character in *Manon* sing-songs a ditty that begins "*Dig et dig et don*" ("Ding and ding and dong")?

12. In what Mozart opera does a duet about bells discuss potential marital infidelities?

13. In *Les Huguenots,* Saint-Bris describes a church bell that will ring twice. Where is that bell situated?

14. What instrument shall soon sound "ding dong," according to the Madrigal in *The Mikado?*

15. In *Cendrillon,* who is frightened but then comforted by the sound of bell chimes?

Extra Credit:

A. In 1982, a long-lost "carillon" was restored to Act II of an Offenbach work performed by the New York City Opera—the first time that bell music had been heard since the show's 1867 world premiere. Name the operetta.

B. In *Il Campanello di Notte,* Enrico rings the apothecary's bell three times. What are his three requests?

C. What three characters sing the bell trio in *H.M.S. Pinafore?*

120. IN STITCHES

Behind the scenes, opera performance involves the skills of many, many untold seamstresses and tailors. But sometimes needlework does make its way into the spotlight!

1. What motif is embroidered on the Boy's jersey in *Peter Grimes?*

2. Who sewed it on?

3. In *The Saint of Bleecker Street,* for what event are stars sewn onto Concettina's "angel dress"?

4. In what opera does an English tailor veto sewing a zipper into a pair of trousers?

5. In *Princess Ida,* who picks up the male impostors' dropped etui that contains "scissors, needles and—cigars"?

6. About what bride is sung, "If her dress is badly fitting / Theirs the fault who made her trousseau"?

7. In what opera does a small chorus of students and seamstresses laugh at a leading character?

8. One scene in *Louise* takes place at a dressmaker's. Which seamstress has lost her scissors?

9. Which seamstress in the same opera demonstrates how to insert whalebone?

10. In Gounod's *Faust,* which song of Marguerite's is also called "The Spinning Wheel Song"?

11. Which rustic player in *A Midsummer Night's Dream* is a tailor?

12. What German opera contains a "Spinning Chorus"?

13. In what twentieth-century opera does the song in question 12 feature strongly?

14. What is the color of the scarf Mrs. Lovett knits for Toby?

15. In *Lizzie Borden,* an important prop is a large tapestry that the title character is embroidering. What does it depict?

Extra Credit:

A. What two fabrics does Mimi say she employs in her needlework?

B. What two flowers does she say she makes?

C. In what opera does one character throw over the martyrdom of "Darn and wash and patch"?

121. TURN OF THE CENTURY, PART I

Below at left is a list of twentieth-century operas that are based upon plays, stories, poems, or novels of a previous era. Can you match the opera titles to their composers or original sources? Double your points by linking all three columns correctly.

A. *Sir John in Love*
B. *Wuthering Heights*
C. *Betrothal in a Monastery*
D. *Gianni Schicchi*
E. *Candide*
F. *Don Quichotte*
G. *The Gambler*
H. *Albert Herring*
I. *Billy Budd*
J. *The Ghosts of Versailles*
K. *Riders to the Sea*
L. *The Mighty Casey*
M. *The Aspern Papers*
N. *Lodoletta*
O. *Der Geburtstag der Infantin*

1. Sergei Prokofiev
2. Giacomo Puccini
3. Jules Massenet
4. William Schuman
5. Pietro Mascagni
6. Carlisle Floyd
7. Ralph Vaughan Williams
8. John Corigliano
9. Alexander von Zemlinsky
10. Leonard Bernstein
11. Benjamin Britten
12. Domenick Argento

a. Herman Melville
b. Voltaire
c. William Shakespeare
d. Ouida
e. Miguel de Cervantes
f. Emily Brontë
g. Ernest Lawrence Thayer
h. Dante Alighieri
i. Oscar Wilde
j. Richard Brinsley Sheridan
k. Henry James
l. Dostoyevsky
m. J. M. Synge
n. Pierre Augustin de Beaumarchais
o. Guy de Maupassant

122. TURN OF THE CENTURY, PART II

OK, it's just gotten harder—or, perhaps, easier. Following the rules of Part I, match these twentieth-century works to their composers and twentieth-century literary sources.

A. *A Question of Taste*
B. *Emmeline*
C. *Transformations*
D. *The Insect Comedy*
E. *Patience and Sarah*
F. *Das Verratene Meer*
G. *Roman River*
H. *Regina*
I. *My Heart's in the Highlands*
J. *Summer and Smoke*
K. *Show Boat*
L. *A Wrinkle in Time*
M. *The Midnight Angel*
N. *Mrs. Dalloway*
O. *The Making of the Representative for Planet 8*

1. Philip Glass
2. Libby Larsen
3. Marc Blitzstein
4. Jack Beeson
5. Tobias Picker
6. Hans Werner Henze
7. Conrad Susa
8. Robert Ward
9. Paula M. Kimper
10. David Carlson
11. Lee Hoiby
12. Jerome Kern
13. Martin Kalmanoff
14. William Schuman

a. Edith Wharton
b. Judith Rossner
c. Isabel Miller
d. Tennessee Williams
e. Edna Ferber
f. Karel Čapek
g. Roald Dahl
h. Virginia Woolf
i. Lillian Hellman
j. William Saroyan
k. Doris Lessing
l. Peter Beagle
m. Anne Sexton
n. Yukio Mishima
o. Madeleine L'Engle

123. THREE TENORS...AND OTHER SINGERS

If the 1980s was the Decade of the Directors, surely the 1990s have turned out to be the Decade of the Singers.

1. Hyped as the next-generation successor to the "Three Tenors," Roberto Alagna has made as much news for his romance with a Romanian colleague as for his voice. Name her.

2. What did they sing together at a Met gala the evening following their marriage?

3. On 12/1/94, the Act I love duet of a newly restaged Met *Madama Butterfly* was disrupted by a most distinguished booer. Who was she?

4. What American soprano, winner of the 1990 Richard Tucker Grand Award, has made the Countess Almaviva something of a signature role with which to make her debut at international houses?

5. What role did she create in *The Ghosts of Versailles?*

6. What Welsh baritone, who first appeared on the opera stage in 1990, has made Mozart's Figaro a signature role?

7. Cecilia Bartoli's first operatic appearance was at the age of nine, with the Rome Opera. What role did she sing?

8. What American-born soprano is considered by some to be her immediate rival, especially in the Rossinian repertoire?

9. In what role did Sergei Leiferkus make his U.S. operatic debut?

10. What American soprano, as Goodwill Ambassador for the United Nations High Commission for Refugees, divides her time between the opera stage and refugee camps, undauntedly concertizing in Sarajevo while the city was under siege?

11. Menotti composed *Goya* at the request of what singer?

12. On 4/27/96, operatic history was made when a singer performed two different roles in two different cities in the same opera on the same day. Name the performer.

13. The *AIDS Quilt Songbook* was created at a baritone's request by such composers as Adams, Corigliano, Rorem, Harbison, Hoiby, and Bolcom. The singer who performed in the work's premiere in 1992 sadly passed away in early 1993. Who was he?

14. When Kathleen Battle was dismissed from the Met during their 1994 *La Fille du Régiment,* what soprano took over the role?

15. What Armenian tenor, world-famous for his work in both Italian and Russian repertoire, has also crossed the U.S. in productions of nineteenth-century Armenian composer Tigran Chukhadjian's opera *Anush?*

Extra Credit:

A. Where did the original Carreras-Domingo-Pavarotti concert take place in 1990, and for what occasion?

B. Alfredo Kraus was miffed at being left off the roster of artists who appeared in the opening ceremonies of the 1992 Barcelona Olympics, but he could take some comfort in the fact that Pavarotti didn't perform there either! Name the six opera singers who did.

C. On 12/31/94, New York's opera-loving Mayor Giuliani made his Met debut in *Die Fledermaus,* joining several of its male stars in a handkerchief-waving rendition of a favorite song of the Big Three. What did they sing?

124. HOT KNIGHTS

Many operas owe their existence to the romance of chivalry—or should we say a lust-filled lack of it? Decide for yourself:

1. The leading lady of *Genoveva* struggles to maintain her virtue while her husband is away on a Crusade. What is his name?

2. In what Rossini opera does a group of women struggle to maintain their virtue until their men return?

3. In Verdi's *Aroldo,* the title character returns from the Crusades to learn his wife has been seduced by a knight. Name her lover.

4. In *Esclarmonde,* a bishop threatens a knight with eternal damnation if he does not break his oath to the eponymous Byzantine sorceress. Who is this stalwart hero?

5. In Gluck's *Armide,* the sorceress of that title plots with a man of royalty to kill the knight, Renaud. Name the blue-blooded bad guy.

6. What Cherubini opera concerns the defeat of a Moorish warrior by Spanish knights in 1492?

7. Influenced by the principles of William Morris, what English composer wrote a five-opera Arthurian cycle?

8. For valiant service against the infidels, what operatic knight is proclaimed both Comte de Zamora and Marquis de Montréal by the very king he is cuckolding?

9. Who created the role of the Green Knight in Birtwistle's 1991 *Gawain?*

10. In Gounod's last opera, Ben Said, a Moorish commander, has defeated the Spanish only to be murdered by a woman—the mother of a slave girl he has bought at auction! What is the title of this work?

11. In what opera does a Saracen order the Arab invasion of Spain to avenge the rape of his daughter by the title character, the country's last Visigoth king?

12. In *I Lombardi,* Griselda falls in love with an infidel. What is his name?

13. In what Bellini opera does a young Christian captive become the fiancée of a sultan, against her will?

14. In what other opera did Bellini employ much of the same music?

15. Did we say "hot"? In what bel canto opera does the King of Portugal free a Moslem girl from the Moors, only to die with her when their ropes are set afire as they flee the Tower of Lisbon together?

Extra Credit:

A. In the 1820s, Donizetti wrote not one, but two operas based on the same eighteenth-century text as was employed by Cherubini, as noted in question 6. What were their titles?

B. Name the six tenor roles in Rossini's *Armida*.

C. Why was the audience shocked by the man who made his London debut as Armando in that city's premiere of *Il Crociato in Egitto?*

125. MAGIC WORDS

One often speaks of the magic of opera—here are some examples of magic *in* opera.

1. In what twentieth-century American opera is one aria totally comprised of a list of folk superstitions?

2. What operatic character kisses a rabbit's foot to have luck while gambling?

3. What sacred plant does Norma use in her ceremonies?

4. In what Handel opera does a character, based on the historical figure Godfrey of Bouillon, use a magic wand to turn an enchanted garden into a desert?

5. What is the name of the magician in *The Consul?*

6. In *Cendrillon,* where does the Fairy Queen live?

7. How is Faust able to fly, in *Mefistofele?*

8. In Gilbert and Sullivan's *The Sorcerer,* how is the love philtre administered?

9. What is John Wellington Wells's address?

10. What is the name of the witch in *Mireille?*

11. Who turned Godfrey of Brabant into a swan?

12. In *Das Rheingold,* what is the first creature that Alberich transforms himself into, at Loge's request?

13. In *Le Postillon de Longjumeau,* who read Chappelou's palm before he hwas married?

14. Who accidentally evokes the devil in *Grisélidis?*

15. When Sullivan refused to collaborate with Gilbert on an operetta about a magic lozenge, what composer did the librettist team up with in order to produce *The Mountebanks?*

Extra Credit:

A. In *The Rake's Progress,* Tom must name three cards drawn by Nick in order to break Nick's spell over him. What are his three correct answers?

B. What is the name of the magician in Johan Strauss' *Tausendundeine Nacht* ("1001 Nights")?

C. What does he administer to Suleiman Ben Akbar to cheer him up?

126. FOR THE RECORD

As record collectors prize their more unusual albums, so may a new generation of CD-lovers these little treasures:

1. What American mezzo has recorded an album of trouser roles, collectively titled *Call Me Mister?*

2. Though she never appeared onscreen, the recorded soundtrack for the 1995 movie *Sense and Sensibility* includes an internationally-renowned soprano singing two original songs by Patrick Doyle. Who is she?

3. In 1996, a mother-daughter recording was produced, featuring Montserrat Caballé in that first capacity. Name her talented offspring.

4 With what late rock singer did mama share a recording in 1992?

5. What German countertenor has recorded an album of pop classics that includes "Lili Marleen" (sic)?

6. What smoky-voiced British mezzo, accompanied by a jazz quartet, has recorded an album of such numbers as "Miss Otis Regrets"?

7. A 1990 recording of *Kiss Me Kate* is the first to include all the songs and ballet music written for the show. What soprano performs the role of Lilli Vanessi, a.k.a. "Kate"?

8. The 1996 recording of what forgotten 1837 Auber opera includes material later written for that work by Tchaikovsky?

9. In 1993, Lyric Distribution produced a CD set of a 1953 Callas performance that had never been commercially released. What was the opera?

10. In that performance, what other soprano, then just beginning her international career, is preserved for posterity in the secondary role of a priestess?

11. What opera singer has, at last count, racked up over a dozen Grammy Awards, virtually double the total of colleagues such as Domingo and Pavarotti?

12. In 1994, London Records produced the first complete commercial recording to be made since 1969 of what opera, in one of the most complicated audio projects ever?

13. In 1992, Frederica von Stade teamed up with Garrison Keillor on a recording. What was the album called?

14. Joan Sutherland has retired, but that did not stop Richard Bonynge from committing rare French works such as *Le Domino Noir* to CD. Who became his new star soprano?

15. During the 1960s, Richard Bonynge sponsored a young tenor with an unusually high range—actually a baritone singing in head voice. Though a mugging in 1983 damaged his throat, this singer retrained and, in 1993, recorded a CD of English songs as a baritone. Who is he?

Extra Credit:

A. The 1991 recording of the London staged revival of *Carmen Jones* was unusual for its "equal opportunity employment" of both casts' Carmen and Joe. Name the two singers who each recorded a portion of those roles.

B. By an odd coincidence, not only did the Scottish Opera and the English National Opera record *Street Scene* in the same year, but three singers in secondary roles appear in those same roles in both recordings. Name the double-duty artists and their respective roles.

C. Within four years of each other, the New York City Opera and the Scottish Opera recorded markedly different versions of *Candide*. What is oddly *non*coincidental about their choice of conductors, when the albums are viewed in tandem?

127. DOUBLE-BILLS, PART I

Earn double points on these last quizzes of super-difficult opera questions. Part I concerns music, lyrics, and composers.

1. In what language was *Lohengrin* first performed in New York?

2. For whom did Massenet rewrite the tenor role of *Werther* for baritone?

3. What name did George Bernard Shaw use when he wrote music criticism?

4. What is Zerbinetta's highest note in R. Strauss's original score for *Ariadne auf Naxos?*

5. What opera requires that a bass sing the role of a character named Bassi?

6. What opera, composed by Kittl, has a text by Richard Wagner?

7. What opera critic wrote the libretto for *Modern Painters?*

8. Who invented the glass armonica, used to chilling effect in *Lucia di Lammermoor?*

9. What composer played Papageno in the first *Die Zauberflöte* to be performed in English in Great Britain?

10. In *Der Rosenkavalier,* who has sent the Italian Singer to perform for the Marschallin?

11. When first presented in London in 1834, a French opera about a Swedish king had a continuous run of 135 performances. What was it?

12. Sullivan wrote the only opera believed to have had a continuous run of over 150 performances. Name it.

13. Better known for his operettas, what composer performed in the orchestra pit of the Met when he first came to America?

14. Tchaikovsky correctly predicted that a French opera—originally a flop—would become one of the world's favorites, and he was right. Which?

15. In what semiautographical opera is a woman so upset over her daughter having an affair with a composer that she kills herself and her amorous child?

Extra Credit:

A. In *Le Postillon de Longjumeau,* what high note of the title character does the Marquis de Corcy specifically compliment?

B. In Act II of *La Bohème,* Schaunard tries out a horn and tells its vendor that a particular note is off. Which note?

C. In *Il Viaggio a Reims,* in what key does the Baron Trombonok ask that the French anthem be sung?

128. DOUBLE-BILLS, PART II

Again, double points for these, concerning opera plots and characters.

1. What opera opens with a description, complete with maps, of one of Napoleon's battles?

2. What brand of matches does Albert Herring seek when he comes home to a dark house?

3. In *L'Etoile du Nord*, Peter the Great—disguised as a humble carpenter—is asked his father's profession. What is his honest reply?

4. Act I of what Zandonai opera is set in a Spanish cigar factory?

5. In what twentieth-century opera is the Hundred Years' War (specifically, during the reign of England's Edward III) reenacted?

6. What phrase does Fiordiligi claim is symbolized by the letters she sees in Dorabella's palm?

7. How is Figaro physically identified as the son of Dr. Bartolo and Marcellina?

8. What sex is Mélisande's child?

9. In what Rossini opera does an aria list such motley items as pearls, trombones, opium, and sables?

10. What college did Kitty attend in *The Last Savage?*

11. What is the name of the eunuch in *Antony and Cleopatra?*

12. In what Saint-Saëns opera does a man fall in love with a woman depicted on a Japanese scroll painting?

13. What Sullivan opera contains a lullaby about bacon?

14. What opera, which premiered on NBC-TV in 1961, is about Mormon leader Brigham Young?

15. In *Il Turco in Italia*, what is Don Geronio's horoscope sign?

Extra Credit:

A. What three types of cigars does Minnie offer the men in *La Fanciulla del West?*

B. Mascagni and Erlanger both wrote operatic works based on the writings of author team Erckmann and Chatrian, and each on Jewish subjects. Name the operas.

C. What are the names of The Defendant and The Plaintiff in *Trial by Jury?*

129. DOUBLE-BILLS, PART III

Double points continue, for some tough questions about singers:

1. What strong-voiced British soprano is a passionate follower of wrestling matches?

2. At the 4/7/93 Opera Orchestra of New York concert staging of *Anna Bolena,* what recently-slimmed American soprano sang the title role in a succession of three different, tightly fitted gowns?

3. What young American tenor, in his 1996 New York recital debut, sang as his first encore "Be My Love," complete with an applied Italian accent?

4. What tenor, who sang the first German Calaf, also composed operettas?

5. What French *bariton-martin* created the role of British art critic John Ruskin in the American opera *Modern Painters?*

6. What was unusual about the casting of Siegfried Jerusalem in Lyric Opera of Chicago's 1993–1996 *Ring* cycle?

7. In 1995, what veteran soprano made her feature-film debut in a film adaptation of late-nineteenth-century homesteading tales?

8. What black American soprano was featured on one of a series of "Famous Woman Trading Cards" issued by Ms. Foundation in 1994?

9. What nineteenth-century tenor—who had been a *postillon* himself before his voice was discovered—sang the title role of *Le Postillon de Longjumeau* over twelve hundred times?

10. What Viennese Wagnerian mezzo started out as an Italian-repertoire lyric soprano?

11. What tenor drew some darts for jokingly launching a paper airplane at his Nannetta, Barbara Bonney, during a 1993 Met performance of *Falstaff?*

12. In 1994, what soprano performed the role of Sister Blanche despite being six months pregnant?

13. What tenor was fired by the Houston Grand Opera for refusing to sing Alfredo's offstage lines during the 4/26/94 "*Sempre libera*"?

14. On 4/24/90, what tenor came out of retirement to take part in a gala honoring his nintieth birthday?

15. What does Samuel Ramey's vanity license plate spell out?

Extra Credit:

A. What pair of bass-baritone identical twins have swapped places onstage as the world's most look-alike Don Giovanni and Leporello?

B. What soprano and tenor were born in the same year in Modena, Italy?

C. Well, *Norma* does concern a sisterhood of sorts. What three siblings sang the three leading female roles in Kentucky Opera's April 1991 production?

130. DOUBLE-BILLS, PART IV

And then there are the opera-related curiosities that seem to defy just about any form of categorization. How well do you hold up in the last of our cycle, this "Twilight (Zone) of the Quizzes"?

1. Why did Henry Bishop sue Donizetti over the Mad Scene in *Anna Bolena?*

2. What Handel opera contains fifteen Italian arias and forty-one in German?

3. What famous artist designed the sets and costumes for the original production of *Orphée aux Enfers?*

4. What well-known American bass composed an opera about Jesus called *I Am the Way?*

5. What Rossini opera was presented in Calcutta in 1834?

6. German composer Peter Cornelius wrote an opera based on a play by French dramatist Pierre Corneille. Name the opera.

7. A marriage proposal not in the libretto entered the surtitles of a 9/93 *Tosca*—and the affirmative reply flashed on-screen during the November *Hänsel und Gretel*—at what U.S. opera house?

8. Rossini made his stage debut singing in an opera by what composer?

9. In what early Verdi opera does a Protestant minister offer his unfaithful wife a divorce?

10. What Richard Strauss opera is based on a work by Ben Jonson?

11. What Donizetti opera contains a national anthem that didn't exist as such during the period of the opera's setting?

12. The operas *Maria di Rudenz* and *Maria di Rohan* have different libretti—by the same librettist. Name him.

13. Manuel de Falla composed a marionette opera based upon *Don Quixote*. What is its title?

14. Name the opera Mascagni wrote in honor of Mussolini.

15. In Leroux's original novel, *The Phantom of the Opera*, what opera is underway when the chandelier comes crashing down?

Extra Credit:

A. Who *was* Fiona Macleod, librettist of *The Immortal Hour?*

B. *Die Tote Stadt* has a libretto by two men using the pen name of Paul Schott. Who were they?

C. For what three operas did Sir Cecil Beaton design productions for the Met?

Answers

Scoring:

Unless otherwise noted, score one point per answer in the main section of each quiz, and two points per answer in the extra credit section.

2251 to 3000 points: STANDING ROOM ONLY
You know more about opera than many music professionals! You not only deserve a torn-program confetti salute, but you know what it is!

1501 to 2250 points: BOX HOLDER
While you are clearly a devoted opera attendee or home listener, you still need to get over a few prejudices (hate new music? only consider international-level stars "real" singers?). To be truly rounded, take another look and listen to areas you are deliberately avoiding in the opera world.

751 to 1500 Points: SUBSCRIBER
A good try! You love opera but now need to expand your horizons beyond tried and true works and artists. The first step: explore other operas by composers you enjoy and works written by their contemporaries, open your ears to other singers' interpretations of familiar pieces, and try a "wild card" now and then.

0 to 750 points: MATINEE MAVEN
You enjoy opera as an entertainment, but have just realized how vast and complex the subject is. Take heart! Everyone who scores higher began at your level. How to improve your score: increase your reading and listening in areas that, in these quizzes, have caught your interest. You'll be a buff in no time!

1. ANSWERS

1. Lalo.
2. Montemezzi.
3. Paulus.
4. Donizetti
5. Chabrier.
6. Rossini.
7. Glinka.
8. Musgrave.

9. Delibes.
10. Bizet.
11. Rimsky-Korsakov.
12. Humperdinck.
13. Massenet.
14. Saint-Saëns.
15. Gounod.

Extra Credit:*

A. Boetia.
B. Anne Boleyn *Anna Bolena,* Mary Stuart, *Maria Stuarda,* Elizabeth I *Roberto Devereux,* the Queen of Shemakha *Le Coq d'Or,* the Queen of the Night *Die Zauberflöte,* Cleopatra *Giulio Cesare,* and Juana *La Loca.*
C. *Un Giorno di Regno.*

*Score one point each for each character name in B, two points each for A and C.

2. ANSWERS*

1. a, k
2. f, u
3. c, k
4. e, g
5. n, o
6. l, s
7. q, s
8. i, o

9. u, m
10. j, n
11. j, p
12. d, r
13. b, f
14. v, l
15. a, c

Extra Credit:

A. iv
B. vi
C. i
D. v
E. ii
F. iii

*Score one point each for each letter to questions 1–15.

3. ANSWERS

1.	e	9.	m
2.	d	10.	h
3.	l	11.	e
4.	j	12.	i
5.	i	13.	k
6.	a	14.	f
7.	b	15.	g
8.	c		

Extra Credit:

A. iii
B. i
C. v
D. ii
E. iv

4. ANSWERS*

All were considered failures at their premieres.

Extra Credit:

Menotti's *The Island God* was such a disaster that the composer quickly withdrew and destroyed most of its score. Only several orchestral passages and songs escaped obliteration.

*Score ten points for the answer to the main body of the quiz; five points each for naming the extra credit opera and providing its reason.

5. ANSWERS

1.	f	8.	a
2.	h	9.	b
3.	g	10.	e
4.	m	11.	c
5.	n	12.	j
6.	l	13.	d
7.	i	14.	k

Extra Credit:*

A. They are half-brothers.
B. She is his foster sister.
C. Radmila, Chrusoš and Štáhlav.

*Score one point per correct name in C.

6. ANSWERS

1. k	9. n
2. e	10. i
3. h	11. d
4. a	12. j
5. o	13. m
6. f*	14. g
7. b	15. c
8. l	

Extra Credit:**

1. Elvira is heard singing a brief fragment of a love song that Arturo subsequently sings back to her in full.
2. Rodolfo's friends, calling to him from the street, retreat respectfully to the Café Momus when they learn that he has a lady visitor upstairs.
3. Manon hears the service at St. Sulpice and, inspired by the sound, soon sings her own fervent if somewhat selfish prayer.
4. Mario, undergoing a torture in the next room, calls out his defiance to Scarpia.
5. As Tamino tries to enter the Masonic temple, voices tell him to turn back.
6. Known as the "Siciliana," this is Turiddu's clandestine serenade to Lola.
7. Violetta hears the revelers celebrating the Mardi Gras outside her window as she lies dying.
8. The townpeople gather to help the crew off Otello's ship.
9. Before the title character makes his appearance, an offstage chorus praises the angels.
10. Marguerite's rejection of Faust in her final moments grants her salvation, in the form of a heavenly pronouncement.

11. As Werther dies in Charlotte's arms, her young siblings sing a happy Christmas carol outside.
12. Nadir sings to Leila even as she prepares to spend the night alone in chaste and pious retreat.
13. We have our first taste of Lakmé's high soprano when she begins a prayer from offstage before appearing onstage to complete it.
14. Bacchus calls joyously to Ariadne, who mistakes him for Death coming to release her from her grief.
15. At the opening of the opera, the spirits of wine and beer sing about how they are man's friend, dispelling fatigue and worry.

*Given in its original Sicilian spelling; in some performances the song is sung in Italian instead.
**Score one point per extra credit answer.

7. ANSWERS

1. Rosa Ponselle.
2. Maria Callas.
3. Jan Peerce.
4. Emma Calvé.
5. Nellie Melba.
6. Alma Gluck.
7. Louise Homer.
8. George London.
9. Richard Tauber.
10. Ernestine Schumann-Heink.
11. Jean de Reszke.
12. Marcella Sembrich.
13. Robert Merrill.
14. Alfredo Kraus.
15. Gérald Souzay.

Extra Credit:

A. Franco Zeffirelli.
B. Lorenzo da Ponte.
C. Ruffo Titta.

8. ANSWERS*

In all cases, their libretti were written by their respective composers.

Extra Credit:

A. Colette.
B. Franco Zeffirelli.
C. Peter Pears.

*Score ten points for the correct answer to the main question, two points per A, B, and C.

9. ANSWERS

1. Mohammed.
2. Silver Dollar.
3. Jerome.
4. Feodor.
5. Jemmy.

6. Catalina.
7. Gherardino.
8. Harry.
9. Max.
10. Willie.

Extra Credit:*

Charlotte, Sophie, Hans, Gretel, Karl, Clara, Max, and Fritz.

*Score one point per correct name in the extra credit section.

10. ANSWERS

1. g
2. b
3. h
4. o
5. k
6. m
7. l
8. c

9. e
10. a
11. d
12. n
13. i
14. j
15. f

Extra Credit:*

A. I. iii
    II. iv
    III. i
    IV. ii

B. V. viii
    VI. v
    VII. vi
    VIII. vii

*Score one point for each answer to A and B.

11. ANSWERS

1. Sophocles.
2. Euripides.
3. Tacitus.
4. Homer.
5. Virgil.

6. Euripides.
7. Ovid.
8. Euripides.
9. Ovid.
10. Sophocles.

Extra Credit:*

A.　i. Midas.
　　ii. A fly.
　　iii. A laurel tree.
　　iv. A spring.
B. Livy.
C. *The Frogs,* by Aristophanes.

*Score one point per answer to A and C, and two points for B.

12. ANSWERS

1. *Semele.*
2. *Vanessa.*
3. *Tosca.*
4. *Turandot.*
5. *Patience.*
6. *Manon.*
7. *Sweeney Todd.*
8. *Norma.*

9. *Faust.*
10. *Orphée aux Enfers.*
11. *The Gondoliers.*
12. *Das Rheingold.*
13. *Alessandro.*
14. *Cavalleria Rusticana.*
15. *La Muette de Portici.*

Extra Credit:*

Fist, nose, cheeks, bosom, eyes, tongue, foot, throat, face, hair, lip, breast, brow, and heart.

*Score one point per item named.

13. ANSWERS

1. *Paul Bunyan.*
2. *Albert Herring.*
3. *The Mighty Casey.*
4. *Ba-Ta-Clan.*
4 *The Mikado.*
6. *Germania.*
7. *Help, Help, The Globolinks!*
8. *Susannah.*

9. *A Midsummer Night's Dream.*
10. *The Tender Land.*
11. *The Bartered Bride.*
12. *Les Contes d'Hoffmann.*
13. *The Abduction of Figaro.*
14. *La Grand-Duchesse de Gérolstein.*
15. *The Love for Three Oranges.*

Extra Credit:*

A. *The Consul.*
B. *Die Frau ohne Schatten.*
C. *Ariadne auf Naxos.*
D. *Suor Angelica.*
E. *Wozzeck.*
F. *Postcard from Morocco.*

*Score one point per correct answer.

14. ANSWERS

1. Richard Dauntless.
2. Act III.
3. Act II.
4. Act III.
5. A minuet.
6. *Der Zigeunerbaron.*
7. A mazurka.
8. A waltz.

9. Jack Point.
10. A galop.
11. A minuet.
12. A polka.
13. A furiant.
14. A gavotte.
15. A minuet.

Extra Credit:*

A. A fandango, quadrille, pavanella, gavotte, and minuet.
B. A polka, barn dance, slow waltz, and hornpipe.
C. A pavane, galliard, and lavolta.

*Score one point for each correctly named dance.

15. ANSWERS

1. j	9. i
2. f	10. b
3. l	11. n
4. a	12. m
5. g	13. e
6. o	14. k
7. d	15. h
8. c	

Extra Credit:

A. *Billy Budd* (his co-librettist was Eric Crozier).
B. W. H. Auden.
C. Gian Carlo Menotti.

16. ANSWERS

1. Thirty-six.
2. Eight (he's allowed seven free).
3. These are the men whose names are cried out by the women who look out their windows during the Act II melee.
4. Woglinde in *Das Rheingold*.
5. Alberich in *Das Rheingold*.
6. Tristan in a Germanic "Ahoy!"
7. *Der Fliegende Holländer*.
8. Nothung.
9. Holda, goddess of spring.
10. Alberich.
11. Grimhilde.
12. The dead warriors strapped to their backs were enemies.
13. His father, Gamuret.
14. *Die Feen*.
15. His back.

Extra Credit:*

A. h	D. g
B. d	E. b
C. i	F. a

G. j   J.   e
H. l   K.   f
I.   k   L.   c

*Score one point per answer.

17. ANSWERS

1. *Aaron Copland.*
2. *Rigoletto.*
3. *Les Troyens.*
4. *Der Fliegende Holländer.*
5. *Lucia de Lammermoor.*
6. *Die Walküre.*
7. *Otello.*
8. *Peter Grimes.*
9. *La Cenerentola.*
10. *La Faniculla del West.*

Extra Credit:

A. *L'Eclair* (The Lightning Bolt) by Halévy, composer of *La Juive.*
B. *Intermezzo* by Richard Strauss.
C. *Lodoletta* by Mascagni.

18. ANSWERS

1. *Falstaff.*
2. *Turandot* (unfinished).
3. *Carmen.*
4. *Les Contes d'Hoffmann* (unfinished).
5. *The Story of a Real Man.*
6. *Guillaume Tell.*
7. *The Emerald Isle* (unfinished).
8. *I Puritani.*
9. *Parsifal.*
10. *L'Africaine.*
11. *Death in Venice.*
12. *Die Zauberflöte.*
13. *Yolanta.*
14. *Capriccio.*
15. *Le Coq d'Or.*

Extra Credit:*

Don Pasquale, Maria di Rohan and, lastly, *Dom Sébastien* (all 1843).

*Score one point per extra credit title, two points for knowing which was the last work; also, one extra point for each correctly guessed "unfinished" of the main section of the quiz.

19. ANSWERS*

The answers are given in this order: composer/lyricist.

1. Rodgers/Hammerstein.
2. Bernstein/Sondheim.
3. G. Gershwin/I. Gershwin and Heyward.
4. Rodgers/Hammerstein.
5. Lerner/Loewe.
6. Porter/Porter.
7. Loesser/Loesser.
8. Rodgers/Hammerstein.
9. Bernstein/Wilbur, LaTouche and Sondheim.
10. Wright/Forrest.
11. Lerner/Loewe.
12. Wright/Forrest.
13. Adler/Ross.
14. Rodgers/Hammerstein.
15. Sondheim/Sondheim.

Extra Credit:

A. Lawrence A. and Mae Wien.
B. B. G. DeSylva.
C. Dorothy Parker.

*Score one point per composer or individual lyricist in main body of the quiz (total possible: thirty-three points); two points per extra credit question.

20. ANSWERS

1. The Duke of Mantua.
2. Edgardo.
3. Hoffmann.
4. Le Comte des Grieux.
5. Elisabetta.
6. Marguerite.
7. Figaro.
8. Giorgio Germont.
9. Sarastro.
10. Roméo.

Extra Credit:*

The original singers, Giulia Grisi (Elvira), Giovanni-Battista Rubini (Arturo), and Antonio Tamburini and Luigi Lablanche (the two Walton brothers) became so famous for their roles that they were known thereafter as the *"Puritani* Quartet."

*One point per singer name, one point per role name.

21. ANSWERS

1. *Les Troyens.*
2. Teatro Amazonas (where Caruso is mistakenly believed to have performed—the closest he ever got was to visit the town in which it is located).
3. 1992.
4. *The Bartered Bride,* which even then had occurred in late morning due to civil defense curfews.
5. Lyons.
6. Italy.
7. The United States (Chicago).
8. Rotterdam, where the opera received its world premiere in 1980 by the Netherlands Opera.
9. Leonard Balada's *Christóbal Colón.* (The tenor was José Carreras, who needed the time to recover from leukemia.)
10. *Die Lustige Witwe.*
11. Pesaro.
12. Puccini.
13. Donizetti's *Otto Mesi in Due Ore.*
14. Finland's Suomalailen Ooppera.
15. *Madama Butterfly.*

Extra Credit:*

A. *Die Fledermaus, Die Lustige Witwe,* and *Die Csárdásfürstin.*
B. *Boris Godunov, Eugene Onegin, The Queen of Spades, War and Peace,* and *The Gambler.*
C. *Macbeth, La Bohème, La Cenerentola,* and *Simon Boccanegra.*

*Score one point per title.

22. ANSWERS

1. Ruggero.
2. Amilcare.
3. Daniel.
4. Bedrich.
5. Riccardo.

6. Umberto.
7. Vincenzo.
8. Mikhail.
9. Gaetano.
10. Emmerich.

Extra Credit:

A. Jakob Liebmann Meyer Beer.
B. Elias Lévy.
C. Gioacchino.

23. ANSWERS

1. Adelina Patti.
2. *"Non più andrai"* from *Le Nozze di Figaro.*
3. "The Groves of Blarney" (better known as "The Last Rose of Summer").
4. "The Star-Spangled Banner."
5. *La Traviata.*
6. *"La blondina in gondoletta."*
7. *Orfeo ed Euridice ("Che farò senzo Euridice").*
8. *"Notte e georno faticare"* from *Don Giovanni.*
9. *H.M.S. Pinafore.*
10. *"Ich grolle nicht."*

Extra Credit:*

A. Giuseppe Sarti's *Fra i Due Litiganti* and Vicente Martín y Soler's *Una Cosa Rara.*
B. "Hail to the school that floats the banner blue" is the song of New York City's Julia Richmond High School.
C. *Monsieur Choufleuri.*

*Score one point each for composers' names and opera titles in A, two points each for B and C.

24. ANSWERS

1. *Fidelio.*
2. *Il Barbiere di Siviglia.*
3. *Martha.*
4. *Ruddigore.*
5. *La Cenerentola.*

6. *Roberto Devereux.*
7. *H.M.S. Pinafore.*
8. *The Gondoliers.*
9. *The Pirates of Penzance.*
10. *Zar und Zimmerman.*

Extra Credit:*

A. Busoni's *Arlecchio.*
B. Auber's *Fra Diavolo.*
C. *"La Prise de Troie"* and *"Les Troyens à Carthage."*

*Score two points for A and B, one point per title in C.

25. ANSWERS

1. London.
2. Vienna.
3. Venice.
4. Paris.
5. New York.
6. Venice.
7. Zurich.
8. Paris.

9. Vienna.
10. St. Petersburg.
11. Prague.
12. Monte Carlo.
13. Milan.
14. Brussels.
15. Paris.

Extra Credit:

A. Contrary to popular belief, the opera was *Rigoletto.*
B. In NBC-TV's New York studio, from which the opera was broadcast live on Christmas Eve, 1951.
C. At the Teatro San Cassiano in Venice.

26. ANSWERS

1. Chautauqua Institution.
2. Purchase, New York.
3. Peter Sellars.
4. The Santa Fe Opera.

5. New Jersey's Waterloo Festival.
6. The Santa Fe Opera.
7. The Mostly Mozart Festival.
8. Artpark, located in Lewiston, New York.
9. Charleston, South Carolina.
10. *The Ballad of Baby Doe,* which premiered in that city and concerns local history.
11. The company performs at Cooperstown, New York, which is also the home of the National Baseball Hall of Fame.
12. Virginia.
13. *Der Protagonist.*
14. Lake George Opera Festival.
15. New York Grand Opera.

Extra Credit:*

A. *Orlando, Ariodante, Semele,* and *Alessandro.*
B. The U.S. premiere of *La Vera Storia,* plus *Falstaff, Elektra,* and *Tosca.*
C. *Don Giovanni, Le Nozze di Figaro,* and *Così Fan Tutte,* all staged by Peter Sellars.

*Score one point per correct opera title.

27. ANSWERS

1. g
2. m
3. n
4. e
5. j
6. a
7. l
8. b
9. c
10. k
11. d
12. o
13. f
14. h
15. i

Extra Credit:

A. Wolf-Ferrari.
B. Bizet and Lecocq tied.
C. Dr. Mesmer, "father of hypnotism."

28. ANSWERS

1. g
2. j
3. f
4. h
5. a
6. i
7. d
8. b

9. c
10. e
11. l
12. a
13. a
14. e
15. k

Extra Credit:

A. Liling Song.
B. Kim.
C. Madama F. B. Pinkerton (abbreviated, her husband's first two names, Benjamin Franklin, formed a term British audiences found rude, so the letters were reversed).

29. ANSWERS

1. Jessye Norman.
2. Jerry Hadley.
3. Tito Gobbi.
4. Eric Idle.
5. Bonaventura Bottone.
6. Alain Vanzo.
7. *Manon.*
8. *West Side Story.*
9. *Tosca.*

10. Samuel Ramey was Don Giovanni, Ferruccio Furlanetto was Leporello.
11. Carol Burnett.
12. Vincent Price.
13. Francisco Araiza.
14. Rockwell Blake.
15. 1986.

Extra Credit:*

A. The opera was *La Bohème*; the singers/roles as follows:
Allan Monk: Schaunard in both performances.
Italo Tajo: Benoit in both performances, plus Alcindoro in 1982.
Dale Caldwell: Parpignol.
Renata Scotto: Mimi in 1977, Musetta in 1982.
B. *Les Mamelles de Tirésias, Arabella, La Bohème, Die Zauberflöte,* and *Samson et Delila.*

C. Montserrat Caballé, Marilyn Horne, Francisco Araiza, Ruggero Raimondi, and Samuel Ramey.

*Score one point per opera, singer, and role (role points total six).

30. ANSWERS.

1. b
2. h
3. j
4. a
5. l
6. a
7. d
8. m

9. e
10. n
11. f
12. c
13. g
14. i
15. k

Extra Credit:

A. Bizet.
B. Fauré.
C. Saint-Saëns.

31. ANSWERS

1. *The Grand Duke.*
2. *Iolanthe.*
3. *Trial by Jury.*
4. *Patience.*
5. *Princess Ida.*
6. *Ruddigore.*
7. *The Yeomen of the Guard.*
8. *H.M.S. Pinafore.*

9. *The Pirates of Penzance.*
10. *Iolanthe.*
11. *Iolanthe.*
12. *Utopia, Limited.*
13. *Utopia, Limited.*
14. *The Grand Duke.*
15. *Thespis.*

Extra Credit:

A. Tarara, the Public Exploder.
B. "Lalabalele molola lililah kallalale poo."
C. Go-To (if needed, he comes on just before the ensemble, when Ko-Ko enters).

32. ANSWERS

1. DuBose Heyward's *Porgy*.
2. Todd Duncan.
3. Anne Brown.
4. Sidney Poitier.
5. Dorothy Dandridge.
6. The Gershwin estate forbids any other casting.*
7. It is an account of the 1955 Russian tour of the opera, which was performed in English without any available Russian libretto to aid its audiences' understanding!
8. Marian Anderson.
9. Ulrica.
10. Robert McFerrin.
11. Amonasro.
12. Langston Hughes.
13. Henry Davis.
14. *Aida*.
15. Sister Mary Elise of the Sisters of the Blessed Sacrament.

Extra Credit:**

A. Colline *La Bohème*.
B. Amneris *Aida*.
C. Elisabeth *Tannhäuser*.
D. Micaëla *Carmen*.
E. Lampanaio *Manon Lescaut*.
F. Erisbe *Ormindo*.

*A notable exception: The New Zealand opera was permitted to employ Maori singers in their *Porgy and Bess*.
**Score one point for each correct answer.

33. ANSWERS

1. *The Crucible*.
2. *Lost in the Stars*.
3. South Africa.
4. *The Most Important Man*.
5. *La Forza del Destino* (Don Alvaro).
6. *The Emperor Jones*.

7. Eugene O'Neill.
8. Lawrence Tibbett.
9. Texarkana, Texas.
10. *Treemonisha.*
11. Her adopted mother, Monisha, found her beneath a tree.
12. Bags of luck.
13. *Satyagraha.*
14. Auber's *Manon Lescaut.*
15. Gomes's *Lo Schiavo.*

Extra Credit:

A. The Amato Opera.
B. Paul Robeson.
C. *A Guest of Honor.*

34. ANSWERS

1. *The Passion of Jonathan Wade.*
2. Lucas Wardlow.
3. *The Ice Break.*
4. *Four Saints in Three Acts.*
5. Spain.
6. Adah le Clerq.
7. Julie.
8. Thea Musgrave. The opera is *Harriet: The Woman Called Moses.*
9. *Troubled Island.*
10. William Grant Still.
11. Jean Jacques Dessalines.
12. The opera *X* was composed by Anthony Davis.
13. His cousin, Thulani Davis.
14. Ben Holt.
15. Kathleen Battle.

Extra Credit:

A. Thomas Bowers.
B. Sissieretta Jones.
C. Caterina Jarlboro, in Chicago Opera Company's 1933 *Aida.*

35. ANSWERS

1. Portsmouth, England.
2. The first person he sees when he lands safely. Unfortunately, this turns out to be his own son.
3. The *Seagull*.
4. Cape Finisterre, owned by the French.
5. The Lake of the Four Cantons.
6. The *Sakol* ("Falcon").
7. The *Santa Rosalia*.
8. Silvano.
9. Ligunia.
10. *Hecate*.
11. Galicia.
12. The *Cotton Blossom*.
13. Sandwyk.
14. Captain Corcoran.
15. *La Gioconda*.

Extra Credit:*

A. Lord Nelson's *H.M.S. Victory*.
B. *H.M.S. Semaphore*. He needed something to rhyme with "more."
C. Cunard and P & O.

*Score one point for each correct answer to A, and two points each for B and C.

36. ANSWERS

1. Cimarosa.
2. R. Strauss.
3. Liszt.
4. Catalani.
5. Massenet.
6. Donizetti.
7. Paderewski.
8. Gounod.
9. J. S. Bach.
10. Borodin.
11. Ravel.
12. Meyerbeer.
13. Spontini.
14. Respighi.
15. Menotti.

Extra Credit:*

A. Boieldieu's *La Dame Blanche*, Donizetti's *Lucrezia Borgia*, and Nicolai's *Die Lustigen Weiber von Windsor*.

B. Bizet's *Les Pêcheurs de Perles.*
C. *Diana von Solange.*

*Score one point for each opera in question A, and two points each for the answers to B and C.

37. ANSWERS

1. 1935.
2. Sylvia McNair.
3. Rockwell Blake.
4. The Opera Company of Philadelphia.
5. All are winners of the Naumberg Competition
6. *The Consul.*
7. William Schuman.
8. *The Crucible.*
9. Ben Heppner.
10. Leontyne Price.

Extra Credit:*

A. Gian Carlo Menotti, for *The Consul* and *The Saint of Bleecker Street.*
B. Anna Kaskas and Arthur Carron.
C. Istanbul.

*Score one point for each correct answer to A and B, and two for C.

38. ANSWERS

1. h
2. j
3. f
4. k
5. a
6. k
7. d
8. e
9. l
10. c
11. e
12. b
13. i
14. g
15. i

Extra Credit:

A. *Madera, Reno, Cypro,* and *Siracusa.* The last proves fatal.
B. *La Périchole.*
C. *La Grande-Duchesse de Gérolstein.*

39. ANSWERS

1. m	9. n
2. a	10. j
3. f	11. e
4. j	12. d
5. c	13. l
6. k	14. l
7. b	15. g
8. h	

Extra Credit:

A. Don Giovanni D'Aragona.
B. *The Libertine.*
C. He was a tenor in its chorus.

40. ANSWERS

1. b	6. d
2. i	7. j
3. e	8. c
4. a	9. g
5. h	10. f

Extra Credit:

A. Schoenberg's *Erwartung.*
B. Smetana.
C. *From the House of the Dead.*

41. ANSWERS

1. f	6. h
2. e	7. d
3. h	8. g
4. e	9. a
5. b	10. c

Extra Credit:

A. *I Due Foscari.*
B. Weber began it, Mahler finished it.
C. Four.

42. ANSWERS

1. Francis Hopkinson's *The Temple of Minerva*, staged in 1781.
2. Francis Hopkinson.
3. Rossini's *Il Barbiere di Siviglia* (it was done in English nine years earlier).
4. James H. Mapleson.
5. George Frederick Bristow's *Rip Van Winkle*.
6. William Henry Fry's *Leonora*.
7. New Orleans.
8. P. T. Barnum.
9. Howard Hanson.
10. *Merry Mount*.

Extra Credit:

A. Annie Louise Cary, who sang Ortrud in 1877.
B. *Cabildo*.
C. *Hänsel und Gretel*.

43. ANSWERS

1. Poker.
2. Faro.
3. Faro.
4. Trina.
5. Three aces and a pair.
6. Seven.
7. Four (Mercedes has three read).
8. The ghost of the Countess.
9. Dominoes.
10. His horses and armor.
11. Robert, sent on a wild goose chase, has not shown up for the match; the Prince wins by default.
12. Skat.
13. Zara.
14. 100 zecchini.
15. Routellenberg.

Extra Credit:

A. Three shillings (or, in modern terms, thirty-six pence).
B. *La Fanciulla del West.*
C. Poussette bets on Guillot, Javotte on the Chevalier des Grieux.

44. ANSWERS

1. f		6. a
2. d and g		7. j
3. g and h		8. e
4. b		9. c
5. b		10. i

Extra Credit:

A. Elisabeth Billington.
B. Louis XVI.
C. *The Gondoliers*...and she *was* amused.

45. ANSWERS

1. i		9. e
2. k		10. g
3. a		11. n
4. o		12. h
5. j		13. l
6. b		14. d
7. m		15. f
8. c		

Extra Credit:

A. Patrick Honoré Bégearss *The Ghosts of Versailles.*
B. Offenbach's *Barkouf.*
C. Honegger wrote the middle three acts; Ibert, I and V.

46. ANSWERS

1. Eight.
2. Lorin Maazel.
3. José van Dam.
4. James Levine.
5. *And the Ship Sails On.*
6. *Fitzcarraldo.*
7. Kathryn Harrold.
8. Francesco Rosi.
9. Three hundred minutes (five hours).
10. *Moonstruck.*
11. *Apocalypse Now.*
12. *The Witches of Eastwick.*
13. *Distant Harmony.*
14. *The Mikado.*
15. *Madama Butterfly* (lent by the San Francisco Opera; the singers, however, were New York City Opera artists).

Extra Credit:*

Bill Bryden, Nicolas Roeg, Charles Sturridge, Jean-Luc Godard, Julien Temple, Bruce Beresford, Robert Altman, Franc Roddam, Ken Russell, and Derek Jarman.

*Score one point apiece.

47. ANSWERS

1. Wilhelmenia Wiggins Fernandez.
2. *"Ebben, ne andrò lontana"* from *La Wally.*
3. *La Traviata.*
4. San Francisco Opera.
5. Best Feature-Length Documentary.
6. *Meeting Venus.*
7. Kiri Te Kanawa.
8. *Tannhäuser.*
9. *Farinelli.*
10. Philip Glass.
11. Ying Huang.

12. *Immortal Beloved.*
13. Gary Oldman.
14. *The Mozart Brothers.*
15. *Don Giovanni.*

Extra Credit:

A. *Farewell My Concubine.*
B. Leslie Cheung.
C. *M. Butterfly* (based on the play of the same name).

48. ANSWERS

1. *Metropolitan.*
2. *San Francisco.*
3. *Naughty Marietta.*
4. *The Great Victor Herbert.*
5. *The Search.*
6. *The Great Waltz* (about Johann Strauss II).
7. Miliza Korjus.
8. *Because You're Mine.*
9. *The Big Broadcast of 1938.*
10. *It's a Date.*
11. *100 Men and a Girl.*
12. He played both Tonio and Silvio.
13. *I Dream Too Much.*
14. *Song O' My Heart.*
15. Gertrude Lawrence.

Extra Credit:*

A. Bruce Dargavel.
B. Monica Sinclair.
C. Dorothy Bond.
D. Margherita Grandi.
E. Hoffmann was both acted and sung by Robert Rounseville.
F. Antonia was both acted and sung by Ann Ayars.

*Score one point apiece.

49. ANSWERS

1. Seven.
2. Two months.
3. Five.
4. One thousand.
5. One year.
6. One year.
7. Seven years.
8. Twenty-seven years.
9. Twenty-five years.
10. One hundred.
11. Fourteen weeks.
12. Thirty.
13. Thirty-two.
14. Three.
15. *The Last Savage.*

Extra Credit:

A. *L'Enfant et les Sortilèges.*
B. The Greek letter pi (π).
C. Major-General Stanley.

50. ANSWERS

1. *Capriccio.*
2. *Daphne* and *Ariadne auf Naxos.*
3. *Louise.*
4. Boleslao Lazuski.
5. Stolz's *Zwei Herzen im Dreivierteltakt* (Two Hearts in Three-Quarter Time).
6. *The Man Who Mistook His Wife for a Hat.*
7. *Help, Help, The Globolinks!*
8. *The Consul.*
9. Mabel Mercer.
10. *Ein Walzertraum.*
11. *The Last Savage.*
12. *The Little Sweep.*
13. *Palestrina.*
14. *The Last Savage.*
15. *The Aspern Papers.*

Extra Credit:

A. *Il Viaggio a Reims.*
B. Fiando Fiorinelli.
C. Alcazar.

51. ANSWERS

1. *Ermione.*
2 "*Cessa di piu resistere*" from *Il Barbiere di Siviglia.*
3. *Il Viaggio a Reims.*
4. *La Gazza Ladra.*
5. *Aureliano in Palmira.*
6. *Elisabetta, Regina d'Inghilterra.*
7. Tancredi's "*Dolce d'amor parole.*"
8. *La Gazzetta.*
9. *Elisabetta, Regina d'Inghilterra.*
10. *Le Comte Ory.*
11. *La Cambiale di Matrimonio.*
12. *L'Occasione Fa il Ladro.*
13. *La Cambiale di Matrimonio.*
14. *Aureliano in Palmira.*
15. *Tancredi.*

Extra Credit:

A. *Bellezza e Cuor di Ferro* ("The Beauty and Heart of Ferro").
B. *Le Passage de la Mer Rouge* ("The Crossing of the Red Sea").
C. *L'Occasione Fa il Ladro.*

52 ANSWERS

1. The Coliseum, home of the English National Opera.
2. Sadler's Wells Opera.
3. All operas performed by the English National Opera are sung in English (the Royal Opera does employ English subtitles to aid in audience understanding of their works).
4. Glyndebourne.
5. John Christie.
6. Sir Rudolf Bing.
7. Three, successively built in the same vicinity after each previous theater burned down. The present theater opened in 1858.
8. 1968.
9. *Ivanhoe.*
10. *The Siege of Rhodes,* which premiered in 1656. It was written by five composers, and featured in its cast the first woman to appear on public stage in England.

11. The Earl of Harewood.
12. *The Love for Three Oranges.*
13. Opera North.
14. The Welsh National Opera.
15. *Le Nozze di Figaro.*

Extra Credit:*

A. The festival was founded by frequent collaborators Benjamin Britten, Peter Pears, and Eric Crozier. Aldeburgh was Britten's hometown.
B. The Beecham Opera Company, which was founded in 1910 and folded in 1919.
C. Walpole.

*Score one point for each founder and final question in A, two points each for the answers to B and C.

53. ANSWERS

1. i	9. a
2. g	10. c
3. b	11. d
4. f	12. e
5. j	13. h
6. d	14. e
7. i	15. k
8. i	

Extra Credit:*

A. Le Bal Musard, Frascati's, Cadet's, Pré Catelan, and Bullier's.
B. *Chérubin.*
C. The Garter Inn, in *Falstaff.*

*Score one point for each correct name in A, and two points each for answers to B and C.

54. ANSWERS

1. A ring.
2. 100 yen.
3. Two florins.
4. 50,000 marks.
5. One zecchin.
6. $1.50.
7. $4.
8. Quattro droppie.

9. 10,000 marks.
10. 100 scudi.
11. 30,000 livres.
12. The title to Gaunersdorf.
13. A ring.
14. 50 ducats.
15. Alice, in *Falstaff*.

Extra Credit:

A. Andrew Borden in *Lizzie Borden*.
B. *Porgy and Bess* (the dead man is Robbins).
C. Leo Fall.

55. ANSWERS

1. d
2. a
3. f
4. b
5. c

6. h
7. e
8. d
9. i
10. g

Extra Credit:

A. *Akhnaten*.
B. *Capriccio*.
C. *Summer and Smoke*.

56. ANSWERS

1. n
2. o
3. e
4. h
5. m
6. j
7. f
8. l

9. d
10. g
11. i
12. b
13. k
14. c
15. a

Extra Credit:

A. Barber.
B. Britten.
C. Bernstein.

57. ANSWERS

1. Eighty-six.
2. Eighty-five.
3. Ninety-five.
4. Eighty-one.
5. Eighty-one.

6. Ninety-three.
7. Eighty-five.
8. Eighty-eight.
9. Eighty-eight.
10. Eighty-one.

Extra Credit:

A. Eighty-four.
B. *New Year.*
C. Manuel Rosenthal.

58. ANSWERS

1. Lily Holmes.
2. *Il Cappello di Paglia di Firenze* ("The Italian Straw Hat").
3. The Countess's nightcap.
4. La Comtesse de Folleville, in *Il Viaggio a Reims*. She is soon cheered up when one intact hat is brought to her.
5. Eboli, in *Don Carlos*.
6. *La Favorite.*
7. Esclarmonde.
8. Otello throws it down when Desdemona tries to bandage his head with it, and then Emilia takes it.
9. *Don Rodrigo.*
10. *Postcard from Morocco.*
11. Lizzie, in *Lizzie Borden*.
12. An antique cross pendant with a secret compartment.
13. *Gloriana*. Elizabeth I is the hostess with the hissy fit.
14. A necklace of thirty pearls.
15. *Euryanthe.*

Extra Credit:

A. *L'Assedio di Corinto* (at the Teatro alla Scala).
B. Linda Roark-Strummer.
C. *Ariadne auf Naxos*, in keeping with the opera's initial segment being a "rehearsal."

59. ANSWERS

1. *The Consul*—as the Secretary flips through her files looking for the name "Sorel."
2. The other women being deported to America, in Puccini's *Manon Lescaut.*
3. Mignon.
4. Nelly.
5. Gaetano.
6. Pierre.
7. Octavian.
8. Quinquin.
9. Pierce.
10. Edward Fairfax Vere.
11. Tannhäuser.
12. Carlo.
13. Barbara.
14. Steve.
15. Carlotto.

Extra Credit:*

A. Welko, Djura, and Jankel.
B. Sempronio and Tizia, respectively.
C. Ned, Will, Tom, and Isaac.

*Score one point for each correct name.

60. ANSWERS

1. April 1, 1900.
2. February 21, 1965.
3. December 1, 1299.
4. February 29.
5. 1940.
6. 1797.
7. 1860.
8. December 26, 1774.

9. April 1899.
10. June 1794.
11. 1647.
12. April 17, 1860.

13. 1414.
14. 452 A.D.
15. 1900.

Extra Credit:

A. The Year of the Tiger, in which the opera is set.
B. December 24, 1856.
C. *Monsieur Choufleuri Restera Chez Lui le 24 janvier 1833.*

61. ANSWERS

1. Mariandel.
2. Sister Colette.
3. Leukippos.
4. *Les Mamelles de Tirésias.*
5. 40,049.
6. Valili, a hussar.
7. His employer catches him shaving.
8. *Le Convenienze Teatrali* (sometimes performed as the revised and expanded *Le Convenienze ed Inconvenienze Teatrali,* in which the "woman" appears in an opera-within-the-opera as a man).
9. Antonio.
10. *Casanova.*
11. *Mesdames de la Halle.*
12. Maximilian.
13. Creonte.
14. Bardolph.
15. Flute.

Extra Credit:

A. Jay Reise's *Rasputin.*
B. Marcello.
C. Linfea.

62. ANSWERS

1. A donkey.
2. A lion.

3. The Animal Tamer in *Lulu.*
4. *Of Mice and Men.*

5. *Der Rosenkavalier.*
6. A donkey.
7. Queenie.
8. Marcellina.
9. *La Wally.*
10. *Der Junge Lord.*

11. Sir Arthur Sullivan.
12. A bull.
13. Daniel Webster.
14. He feeds Daniel buckshot to weigh him down.
15. *Candide.*

Extra Credit:

A. Purcell's *King Arthur.*
B. *Gloriana.*
C. Nero.

63. ANSWERS

Each opera has no overture.

Extra Credit:

A. Lully.
B. *The Bartered Bride.*
C. *Aida.*

*Score ten points for the correct answer to the main question, two points per extra credit answer.

64. ANSWERS

1. f
2. c, g
3. f
4. h
5. j
6. d
7. k
8. a

9. b
10. l
11. m
12. i
13. d, j
14. e
15. h

Extra Credit:

A. *La Rondine.*
B. *Four Saints in Three Acts.*
C. Henry Price, who sang the role of St. Chavez.

65. ANSWERS

1. Midnight.
2. 7 A.M.
3. 11 P.M.
4. Midnight.
5. Midnight.
6. 10 P.M.
7. 5 A.M.
8. 8:15 P.M.
9. Noon.
10. Midnight.
11. Noon.
12. 9 A.M.
13. 11 A.M.
14. Midnight.
15. 7 P.M.

Extra Credit:

A. Gonzalve and Don Inigo.
B. 7 A.M. to 11 P.M.
C. 2 P.M. to 3 P.M.

*Score one point for each name in A, and two points each for B and C.

66. ANSWERS

1. j
2. e
3. g
4. k
5. a
6. b
7. c
8. l
9. n
10. m
11. h
12. p
13. o
14. d
15. f, i

Extra Credit:

A. *"Parmi veder le lagrime."*
B. Serena.
C. *Treemonisha.*

67. ANSWERS

1. An eagle.
2. A white dove.
3. A jaybird.
4. *Noyes Fludde.*
5. A turtledove.
6. *La Belle Hélène.*
7. *H.M.S. Pinafore.*
8. *Roméo et Juliette.*

9. A parrot.
10. Her Great Auk.
11. Doves.
12. *Sweeney Todd.*

13. The *Tom-Tit.*
14. The Astrologer.
15. *The Yeomen of the Guard.*

Extra Credit:

A. *Lizzie Borden.*
B. *Don Rodrigo.*
C. *The Cunning Little Vixen.*

68. ANSWERS

1. He is wounded by Octavian's sword.
2. To blow a foreign body out of his eye.
3. Mustafa.
4. Paisiello's *Il Barbiere di Siviglia.*
5. *Le Postillon de Longjumeau.*
6. *La Fille du Tambour-Major.*
7. The Offenbach pastiche *Christopher Columbus.*
8. Cholera.
9. Mandryka, after a run-in with a bear.
10. *The Ice Break.*
11. Cholera.
12. *Lucrezia Borgia.*
13. Syphillis.
14. Arsenic.
15. Women of her station don't *need* smelling salts.

Extra Credit:

A. Shirley MacLaine.
B. A veterinarian.
C. *Le Médecin Malgré Lui.*

69. ANSWERS

1. m
2. i
3. e
4. a, g

5. p
6. d
7. j
8. c

9. b
10. f
11. h
12. o

13. k
14. l
15. n

Extra Credit:*

A. Fred Plotkin, who served a number of years as their performance manager.
B. Jerome Hines.
C. *Bubbles: A Self Portrait.*
   Bubbles: An Encore.
   Beverly: An Autobiography.

*Score two points each for A and B, one point for each answer to C.

70. ANSWERS

1. h
2. c
3. a
4. f
5. g

6. b
7. a
8. i
9. e
10. d

Extra Credit:*

A. The book is called *The Blue Aspic,* and its heroine, Ortenzia Caviglia.
B. *Mawrdew Czgochwz.*
C. *Giant's Bread* was the title, Agatha Christie the real author.

*Score one point each for A and C, and two points for B.

71. ANSWERS

1. d
2. i
3. m
4. j
5. l
6. n
7. f
8. k

9. a
10. b
11. o
12. g
13. c
14. h
15. e

Extra Credit:

A. *Louise.*
B. *La Pomme d'Api.*
C. *Zazà.*

72. ANSWERS

1. A telephone.
2. *Les Mamelles de Tirésias.*
3. *The Cradle Will Rock.*
4. A jukebox (the aria really *was* a pop song of the fifties, sung by Mario Lanza).
5. *The Consul.*
6. *Paul Bunyan.*
7. *The Story of a Real Man.*
8. *The Last Savage.*
9. *Four Saints in Three Acts.*
10. *Gallantry.*

Extra Credit:

A. *Einstein on the Beach.*
B. *La Voyage de la Lune.*
C. *Trouble in Tahiti.*

73. ANSWERS

1. General.
2. Corporal.
3. Sergeant.
4. General.
5. Private.
6. General.
7. Lieutenant.
8. Captain.
9. Captain.
10. General.
11. Major.
12. Major.
13. Captain.
14. First Lieutenant.
15. Second Lieutenant.

Extra Credit:*

A. Eddie Perkins.
B. Napoleon III's twenty-first.

C. Gandarte is employed by Poro, an Indian king, while Timagere fights on the side of Alessandro (Alexander the Great). It is interesting to note that the role of all four men were originally written for either soprano or alto.

*Score two points each for A and B, one point for each army affiliation in C

74. ANSWERS

1. f		9. k	
2. d		10. e	
3. a		11. o	
4. n		12. g	
5. b		13. i	
6. j		14. l	
7. m		15. h	
8. c			

Extra Credit:*

A. Ambassador to London.
B. Tsar Ivan, Prince Charles Edward, King Stanislaus, King Hermann Augustus, and Sultan Achmet.
C. Ulric, Prince of Tieffenburg.

*Score one point for each answer to B, two points each for A and C.

75. ANSWERS

1. *La Cenerentola* (Don Magnifico's vision of what meal he will have when a daughter is married to the prince).
2. *The Sorcerer* (the banquet where the philtre is administered).
3. *La Jolie Fille de Perth* (the proposed wedding feast).
4. *Paul Bunyan* (Christmas dinner).
5. *Falstaff* (Falstaff's meal).
6. *Manon* (the offerings at the inn, in Act I).
7. *Hänsel und Gretel* (what Father brings home for supper).
8. *Hänsel und Gretel* (what the Witch promises the children).
9. *Le Jongleur de Notre-Dame* (the meal Boniface prepares).
10. *Suor Angelica* (the foods supporters have brought to the convent).
11. *La Bohème* (Christmas dinner at the cafe).

12. *Albert Herring* (the May Day feast as described by the children).
13. *Albert Herring* (the May Day feast as recalled by Albert).

Extra Credit:

A. *Paul Bunyan.*
B. *Le Docteur Miracle.*
C. *L'Etoile.*

76. ANSWERS

1. k	9. n
2. a	10. e
3. h	11. j
4. m	12. l
5. b	13. i
6. g	14. f
7. l	15. c
8. d	

Extra Credit:*

A. Honan, Kiu, and Tsiang.
B. *La Gioconda.*
C. Puccini's Manon Lescaut, when she's on the verge of being deported there.

*Score one point each for the answers to A, two points each for B and C.

77. ANSWERS

1. A blue handkerchief.
2. Queen Isabella.
3. Ten.
4. Statues of the twelve Apostles.
5. A donkey skin.
6. A gold chain.
7. Madame Armfeldt.
8. The Eusinian Sea.
9. Harry Easter in *Street Scene,* wooing Rose.
10. A bow and arrows.
11. He ordered the streets of Verona to be covered thickly with salt.

12. A ruby clasp.
13. Antonio, her foster father.
14. A handkerchief, accompanied by a card saying it was from her and the man Alma loved.
15. A bracelet.

Extra Credit:*

A. Flowers, perfume, and lace, respectively.
B. Salome (Herod is the man doing the offering).
C. Lady Billows gives him a purse of 25 sovereigns, the Mayor presents Albert with a savings passbook listing a balance of five pounds, and Miss Wordsworth's school sends him Foxes' *Book of Martyrs*—in two volumes, illustrated, inscribed, and dated!

*Score one point for each answer to A and C, two points for B.

78. ANSWERS

1. Sian Edwards.
2. Jean Fournet.
3. Riccardo Muti.
4. Sir Georg Solti.
5. Sir Colin Davis.
6. Eve Queler.
7. John Eliot Gardiner.
8. Rome Opera.
9. Vincent LaSelva.
10. The Met's *Aida*.
11. Alessandro Siciliani.
12. Giuseppe Sinopoli.
13. Kent Nagano.
14. Valery Gergiev.
15. Carlo Rizzi.

Extra Credit:

A. Sarah Caldwell.
B. Bernard Haitink.
C. Wolfgang Sawallisch.

79. ANSWERS

1. Mulberry.
2. A red poppy.
3. Laurel.
4. A lilac bush.
5. Green orchids.
6. Violets.
7. Orchids.
8. An orchid. (Significantly, the Latin root derives from the Greek *orchis,* which means "testicle.")

9. Roses.
10. A datura.
11. Sage.
12. Willow.

13. Balsam.
14. Violets.
15. Edelweiss.

Extra Credit:

A. A thousand-year-old oak branch.
B. *La Jolie Fille de Perth.*
C. It has been scented with oil of roses.

80. ANSWERS

1. Aunt Eth.
2. Ocunama.
3. McKinley.
4. Nina Micheltorena.
5. William Spode.
6. David.
7. Bianca.
8. Radbod.

9. Anna Viola.
10. Tyrone.
11. Bossuet.
12. Idia Legray.
13. The Prince of Conti.
14. Mitzi Mayer.
15. Charlotte Marie Adelaide von Zarkinow.

Extra Credit:*

A. Leonore, Gretchen, and Fausta, respectively.
B. Zerbinetta's old loves.
C. *Patience.*

*Score one point each for answers to A, two points each for B and C.

81. ANSWERS

1. La Scala, in 1969.
2. *Madama Butterfly* at the Met.
3. Peter Sellars.
4. *La Favorite,* at the Teatro La Fenice.
5. The Opera Theatre of St. Louis (the opera was *Così Fan Tutte*).
6. Francesca Zambello.
7. Sarah Caldwell.
8. A 1986 *Carmen* for the Teatro San Carlo.
9. *Faust,* in 1990.

10. Graziella Sciutti.
11. Jean-Pierre Ponnelle.
12. *Carmen* at the Hamburg State Opera.
13. Hope Clarke.
14. Peter Brook.
15. Tito Capobianco.

Extra Credit:

A. Elijah Moshinsky.
B. Lotfollah ("Lotfi") Mansouri.
C. Christopher and David Alden.

82. ANSWERS

1. The Houston Grand Opera.
2. Timothy Nolen.
3. Joaquin Romaguera.
4. Daniel O'Higgins.
5. *A Little Night Music.*
6. Jonathan Tunick.
7. Paul Gemignani.
8. The score is written in, or in variations on, three-quarter time.
9. Mahler.
10. *The Bartered Bride.*
11. Erie Mills.
12. Licia Albanese.
13. English National Opera.
14. "A Stephen Sondheim Evening," recorded at Sotheby's 3/3/83 (the singer was Angela Lansbury).
15. The same as above, in the final selection "Old Friends" (from *Merrily We Roll Along*), which he began singing alone, and which became an ensemble by the entire cast.

Extra Credit:*

A. Mr. Lindquist, Mrs. Nordstrom, Mrs. Anderssen, Mr. Erlanson, and Mrs. Segstrom.
B. Oxford University.
C. Lieutenant Torasso.

*Score one point for each name in A, two points each for B and C.

83. ANSWERS

1. i
2. d
3. g
4. f
5. l
6. m
7. b
8. o

9. n
10. a
11. c
12. h
13. e
14. j
15. k

Extra Credit:

A. The Hildebrands.
B. Lulu.
C. *Andrea Chénier.*

84. ANSWERS

1. *Il Mondo della Luna.*
2. Orff's *Der Mond.*
3 St. Peter.
4. *New Year.*
5. The alcoholic beverage shared by Dick and Mae.
6. Peter Russell.
7 *Minutes Till Midnight.*
8. Blomdahl's 1959 *Aniara.*
9. *The Excursions of Mr. Brouček.*
10. *The Bride From Pluto.*
11. *La Voyage dans la Lune.*
12. *Help, Help, the Globolinks!*
13. Tonal music.
14. Paul Lincke.
15. In a balloon.

Extra Credit:

A. Pooh-Bah.
B. David Henry Hwang and Jerome Sirlin, respectively.
C. *1000 Airplanes on the Roof.*

85. ANSWERS

1. g
2 d
3. b
4. h
.5. a

6. c
7. g
8. e
9. i, j
10. f

Extra Credit:

A. Sister Angela.
B. Saint-Jacques de Compostelle.
C. The Sons and Daughters of Repent Ye Saith the Lord.

86. ANSWERS

1. e
2. c
3. i
4. h
5. a
6. b
7 j
8. k

9. o
10. d
11. f
12. g
13. m
14. l
15. n

Extra Credit:*

A. Clara and Gualtiero.
B. McLean, Ott, Hayes, and Gleaton.
C. Archbishop of Titipu.

*Score one point for each correct name in A and B, two points for C.

87. ANSWERS

1. Antonio Carlos Gomes.
2. Dom Pedro II, Emperor of Peru.
3. The thighbones of their overpowered enemies.
4. Zora.
5. Adolphe Adam.
6. André Grétry.

7. Quechuan.
8. *Natoma.*
9. Polynesia.
10. Argentina.
11. *Azora.*
12. Heitor Villa-Lobos.
13. *Die Schatzkammer des Inka* ("The Incans' Treasure Chest").
14. *The Indian Queen.*
15. Purcell's brother, David.

Extra Credit:

A. Joseph Quesnel's *Colas et Colinette* (1790).
B. Toronto.
C. Montreal (they went on to visit Toronto as well).

88. ANSWERS

1. j	9. k
2. g	10. c
3. a	11. h
4. b	12. m
5. i	13. f
6. l	14. d
7. n	15. e
8. a	

Extra Credit:

A. Schnittke's *Life With an Idiot.*
B. Messager's *L'Amour Masqué.*
C. *L'Enfant et les Sortilèges.*

89. ANSWERS

1. *Lakmé.*
2. *Le Jongleur de Notre-Dame.*
3. *Manon.*
4. *Louise.*
5. Dr. Coppelius, in *Les Contes d'Hoffmann.*
6. Mrs. Herring's greengrocery.

7. *La Bohème.*
8. *Porgy and Bess.*
9. *Street Scene.*
10. *Hugh the Drover.*

Extra Credit:

A. *The Rake's Progress.*
B. *La Forza del Destino.*
C. Ibert's *Angélique.*

90. ANSWERS

1. Berlioz.
2. Gounod.
3. Mozart.
4. Sullivan.
5. R. Strauss.
6. Haydn.
7. Schoenberg.
8. Wagner.

9. Puccini.
10. R. Strauss.
11. Gluck.
12. Offenbach.
13. Verdi.
14. Monteverdi.
15. Handel.

Extra Credit:*

1. Ravel.
2. Bizet.
3. Dvořák.
4. Stravinsky.
5. Henze.
6. E. T. A. Hoffmann.
7. R. Strauss.
8. Berlioz.

9. Shostakovich.
10. Tchaikovsky.
11. Handel.
12. Rossini.
13. Bizet.
14. Stravinsky.
15. Beethoven.

*Score one point each.

91. ANSWERS

1. *The Rake's Progress.*
2. *Maria Stuarda.*
3. *Porgy and Bess.*

4. *Dido and Aeneas.*
5. *Rienzi.*
6. *Les Huguenots.*

7. *Salome.*
8. *La Favorite.*
9. *Guillaume Tell.*
10. *Der Rosenkavalier.*
11. *Götterdämmerung.*

12. *Ernani.*
13. *Don Giovanni* and *Le Nozze di Figaro.*
14. *Pelléas et Mélisande.*
15. *Tristan und Isolde.*

Extra Credit:*

1. Britten.
2. Donizetti himself after its premiere.
3. Thomson.
4. Holst.
5. Sullivan.
6. Schumann.
7. Saint-Saëns.

8. Schumann.
9. Donizetti.
10. Stravinsky.
11. Fauré.
12. Gounod.
13. Beethoven.
14. Fauré.
15. Berlioz.

*Score one point each.

92. ANSWERS

1. d
2. a
3. g
4. h
5. i

6. b
7. d
8. f
9. c
10. e

Extra Credit:*

A. Dame Joan Sutherland.
B. Sir William, Little Billy, and Rudi.
C. Maurice Sendak.

*Score two points each for A and C, one point for each answer to B.

93. ANSWERS

1. Soprano Alwina Valleria, who sang Leonora in *Il Trovatore* during their first season.
2. Mrs. August Belmont.

3. J. P. Morgan.
4. *Hänsel und Gretel,* on 12/25/31.
5. *Il Trovatore.*
6. *Così Fan Tutte.*
7. 10/22/83.
8. 1897–1898, canceled with the death of general manager Henry Abbey. The Met's 1892–1893 had also been canceled, as the result of a fire that had nearly destroyed the house.
9. *Samson et Dalila.*
10. 1/13/10—*Cavalleria Rusticana/Pagliacci.*
11. General manager Giulio Gatti-Casazza.
12. George Cehanovsky.
13. Charles Anthony.
14. "Grand Operatic Surprise Party."
15. Rosina Galli, wife of Giulio Gatti-Casazza.

Extra Credit:*

A. *Orfeo ed Euridice* (1936), *Le Coq d'Or* (1937) and *The Rake's Progress* (1953).
B. *Peter Ibbetson* by Deems Taylor; it was preceded in the afternoon by *Hänsel und Gretel.*
C. 1883–1884 was Italian, 1884–1885 was German.

*Score one point for each correct answer (total seven points).

94. ANSWERS

1. *Rinaldo.*
2. 1995–1996.
3. *Faust,* on 3/10/90.
4. Risë Stevens.
5. *Carmen.*
6. *Madama Butterfly,* shelved with the bombing of Pearl Harbor.
7. 12/29/69, due to a labor strike.
8. Goeran Gentele.
9. *Otello,* on 11/29/48.
10. Avery Fisher Hall, then known as Philharmonic Hall (the program consisted of Falla's *El Amor Brujo* and *Atlantida*).
11. Paata Burchuladze.
12. *La Bohème.*

13. *Fanciulla del West,* given by the company's student artists on 4/11/66 to test the acoustics.
14. Giuseppe Taddei.
15. The Met's summer season at Lewisohn Stadium, inaugurated in 1965.

Extra Credit:*

A. *Lohengrin, Die Meistersinger, Tristan und Isolde, Parsifal,* and the four parts of the *Ring.*
B. *Götterdämmerung* (11/22/63) and *Manon* (11/25/63).
C. *Pagliacci's* Prologue, *La Bohème* Act I, *Il Barbiere di Siviglia* Act II, and *Aida* Act I, Scene 1 and Act II.

*Score one point per opera title (*Ring* and *Aida,* count a total of four and two, respectively) and one point each per name or company title.

95. ANSWERS

1. *La Traviata.*
2. The Fujiwara Opera Company of Tokyo (the two languages were Italian and Japanese).
3. The 1983 Puccini festival.
4. Nicholas Muni.
5. *Crispino e la Comare.*
6. Thea Musgrave, its composer.
7. *Don Giovanni.*
8. *The Tender Land.*
9. Ashley Putnam.
10. *Carmen,* on 10/14/79.
11. 9/2/85.
12. *The Mother of Three Sons.*
13. The Queen of the Night.
14. The L.A.-based Music Center Opera Association, under whose auspices New York City Opera presented operas in Los Angeles.
15. *La Traviata.*

Extra Credit:*

A. Laszlo Halasz, Joseph Rosenstock, Erich Leinsdorf, Julius Rudel, Beverly Sills, Christopher Keene, and Paul Kellogg.

B. *The Student from Salamanca*/Jan Bach.
   Before Breakfast/Thomas Pasatieri.
   Madame Adare/Stanley Silverman.
C. *Griffelkin*/Lukas Foss.
   Marilyn/Ezra Laderman.
   Esther/Hugo Weisgall.

*Score one point for each person or opera title.

96. ANSWERS

1. Louise, in *Louise*.
2. Valzacchi.
3. Abe Kaplan.
4. Two nursemaids who have "gone slumming" to the scene of the crime.
5. *Das Tagblatt*.
6. *"In Paris ist Revolution ausgebrochen"* ("Revolution has broken out in Paris").
7. *Of Mice and Men*.
8. Maria Corona.
9. If she kills someone.
10. Dutch.
11. *Constituzional*.
12. *Castoro*.
13. *La Gazetta*.
14. Bill Zakariesen.
15. Hector Berlioz.

Extra Credit:*

The Times, Tribune, Sun, Herald, and *Clipper*.

*Score one point per correct title.

97. ANSWERS

1. Seventeen
2. Six months
3. Sixteen
4. Eighteen
5. Twelve
6. Twenty-one
7. Forty-seven
8. Twenty

9. Fifteen
10. Fifty
11. Forty-six
12. Thirty-three

13. Eighteen years and two months
14. Ninety
15. Minus eight

Extra Credit:*

A. c
B. d
C. h
D. e
E. f

F. b
G. g
H. a
I. b
J. i

*Score one point per answer.

98. ANSWERS

1. Handball.
2. To retrieve their ball, which had been thrown inside.
3. Five.
4. Cleopatra.
5. *Les Troyens.*
6. *Fedora.*
7. Gounod's *Sapho.*
8. Chess.
9. *Death in Venice.*
10. *La Belle Hélène.*

Extra Credit:*

A. Charlie, Joan, and Willie.
B. Barbamuche.
C. Samuel Barber.

*Score one point for each name in A, two points each for B and C.

99. ANSWERS

1. Roberto Aronica.
2. Ann Murray.
3. Arthur Davies.
4. William Guthrie.
5. Hildegard Behrens.
6. Aprile Millo.
7. Beverly Evans.
8. Eva Marton.

9. Ashley Putnam.
10. Marilyn Mims.
11. Plácido Domingo.
12. Paul Plishka.
13. *La Bohème*.
14. Peter Hofmann.
15. Stanford Olsen.

Extra Credit:*

A. Giuseppe Patané and Eugene Kohn.
B. Neil Shicoff, Neil Rosenshein, and Neil Wilson.
C. When Neil Shicoff lost his voice early in the show, William Lewis—also indisposed vocally—mimed Hoffmann onstage while Kenneth Riegel sang the role from the orchestra pit.

*Score one point for each name.

100. ANSWERS

1. Jean-Luc Viala.
2. Ruth Ann Swenson.
3. Earle Patriarco.
4. Will Roy. They settled for six figures.
5. Stephen Powell.
6. *Idomeneo*.
7. *"Come per me sereno"* from *La Somnambula*.
8. Graham Clark.
9. Cavaradossi.
10. Ben Heppner.
11. Carol Vaness.
12. Diana Soviero.
13. The Frankfurt Opera House (the local opera wags, who had been dissatisfied with the company's new *Ring* that had only just concluded with *Götterdämmerung*, joked that the staging director had *finally* got it right).
14. Barcelona's Gran Teatro del Liceu.
15. Teatro La Fenice in Venice.

Extra Credit:

A. Richard Versalle, who was to die very soon after of the heart attack that had felled him.
B. "Too bad you can only live so long."
C. A blizzard depositing over two feet of snow had paralyzed New York City the day before.

101. ANSWERS

1. *Puss in Boots.*
2. Captain Corcoran.
3. *Macbeth.*
4. Domenico Scarlatti.
5. Aaron Copland.
6. Giulio Gatti-Casazza.
7. Igor Stravinsky.
8. Mezzo.
9. Baritone.
10. Kitty.
11. Marian Anderson.
12. "Cats' Creed."
13. Growltiger.
14. *Tobermory.*
15. Caruso.

Extra Credit:

A. Fido.
B. The Forester.
C. Strohmien (it is amusing to note that, in the libretto, the list of characters in this opera includes a dog, referred to as a "non-singing role."—one hopes so).

102. ANSWERS

1. James Bowman.
2. Paul Esswood.
3. Alfred Deller.
4. Death *The Pardoner's Tale.*
5. Mark Deller.
6. Michael Chance.
7. Randall Wong.
8. Brian Asawa.
9. La Gran Scena Opera Co.
10. Vera Galupe-Borszkh.
11. Brian Asawa.
12. Jochen Kowalski.
13. David Daniels.
14. Keeper of the Threshold *Die Frau ohne Schatten.*
15. Drew Minter.

Extra Credit:*

A. *Giulio Cesare*; Jeffrey Gall and Derek Lee Ragin.

B. Orfeo was composed for castrato, and Orphée for high countertenor.

C. The on-screen actor is Stefano Dionisi; the singing is a high-tech hash of the voices of countertenor Derek Lee Ragin and soprano Ewa Mallas-Godlewska.

*Score one point per correct artist or role, and, in B., *Fach*

103. ANSWERS

1. *The Yellow Wallpaper* (by writer and social reformer Charlotte Perkins Gilman).
2. *Edgar.*
3. Ginastera's *Beatrix Cenci.*
4. Skylight Comic Opera of Milwaukee.
5. San Diego Opera.
6. Washington Opera.
7. *Harvey Milk.*
8. Boston Lyric Opera.
9. Ardis Krainik.
10. Minnesota Opera Theater.
11. *El Gato Montés.*
12. Sarasota Opera.
13. *Dreamkeepers.*
14. Ute Indians.
15. *Guillaume Tell.*

Extra Credit:

A. Dallas (Dallas Opera) and Evanston, Illinois (Northwestern University).
B. *L'Elisir d'Amore.*
C. Tulsa Opera.

104. ANSWERS

1. Marc-Antoine Charpentier.
2. *Atys.*
3. *Serse* (technically, it is a larghetto, and not a largo).
4. The Duke of Athens.

5. *Hippolyte et Aricie* (the "Hippolyte" of the title is Hippolytus, Theseus' son).
6. Marc Minkowski
7. *Titon et l'Aurore.*
8. Conductor-critic Will Crutchfield.
9. Handel's last, *Deidamia.*
10. *Cadmus et Hermione.*
11. Francesco Cavalli (the opera was *Ercole Amante).*
12. Orfeo is torn to bits by the Bacchantes.
13. Voltaire
14. *Artaserse.*
15. Ann Murray.

Extra Credit:

A. Pierre and Thomas Corneille.
B. Both works use the libretto by Thomas Corneille.
C. I. b
  II. a
  III. a
  IV. a
  V. c

105. ANSWERS

1. Edgardo and Lucia.
2. *Don Pasquale.*
3. Her grandmother, the Old Baroness.
4. The Pastor.
5. Seven years.
6. For marrying a mortal. Normally, the punishment is death, but the Fairy Queen commuted her sentence to penal servitude on earth.
7. Carmela and Salvatore.
8. In a game of blindman's buff. Marco snares Gianetta, and Giuseppe captures Tessa.
9. A bouquet of violets.
10. The next day.
11. Sicilian forces begin their massacre of their French invaders.
12. A guest finds the body of Zinovy, Katarina's murdered first husband.
13. The Poles burst into the house and take away Antonida's father.

14. The Willard Hotel in Washington, D.C.
15. Barbara, now wed to Gabrielle, is Casanova's illegitimate daughter. She reveals this secret identity to her father after the toast is concluded.

Extra Credit:*

A. Her white veil, necklace of pearls, and head-wreath of roses. The first item is used for quite another purpose.
B. "Marriage with deceased wife's sister" (this law was overturned in 1907).
C. W. S. Gilbert.

*Score one point for each correct item in A, two points each for B and C.

106. ANSWERS

1. The Harz Mountains.
2. Hungary.
3. Auerbach's Cellar.
4. Helen of Troy.
5. He whistles.
6. An inn in Wittenberg.
7. Baba the Turk.
8. Adonis.
9. Eight engravings by Hogarth.
10. Marbuel.
11. Cologne.
12. Jabez Stone.
13. Ursuline.
14. Brander.
15. Wagner.

Extra Credit:*

A. Gravis, Levis, Asmodus, Beelzebub, and Megaros.
B. Rarach.
C. *The Mother of Us All.*

*Score one point for each correct name in A, two points each for B and C.

107. ANSWERS

1. German.
2. The Hapsburg archduke who became Emperor of Mexico.
3. *Bolivar.*
4. Vasco da Gama.
5. Alberto Franchetti.
6. Greater Miami Opera.
7. *Fernand Cortez.*
8. Offenbach.
9. Downtown Manhattan.
10. Minnehaha.
11. Coca-Cola.

12. *The Voyage.*
13. Donizetti.

14. *La Créole.*
15. *Les Indes Galantes.*

Extra Credit:

A. Turandot.
B. Arturo Toscanini.
C. Don Fernando d'Ibaraa y Figueora y Mascarenes y Lampourdos y Souza.

108. ANSWERS

1. Virgil Thomson.
2. *Man and Superman.*
3. *Arms and the Man.*
4. Heine.
5. *Guglielmo Ratcliffe.*
6 *Mignon.*
7. Voltaire.
8. Cervantes.

9. Schiller.
10. Laclos.
11. Daudet.
12. *The Love for Three Oranges.*
13. Ben Jonson's *Epicoene.*
14. Balzac's *Piene de Coeur d'une Chatte Anglaise.*
15. *Boulevard Solitude.*

Extra Credit:

A. *Il Corsaro* and *I Due Foscari.*
B. *Parisina* and *Marino Faliero.*
C. Jean Cocteau (*Oedipus Rex*).

109. ANSWERS

1. *Die Entführung aus dem Serail.*
2. Salieri's *Prima la Musica e poi le Parole.*
3. Vienna.
4. *Zaïda.*
5. *Mitridate, Rè di Ponto.*
6. Clement XIV.
7. *Il Rè Pastore.*
8. *La Finta Giardiniera.*
9. *Bastien und Bastienne,* based on *Le Devin du Village.*
10. Gluck.
11. Tenor.
12. Idamente, *Idomeneo.*

13. *Don Giovanni.*
14. *La Clemenza di Tito.*
15. *The Jewel Box.*

Extra Credit:

A. Violin.
B. Piano.
C. Maria Anna.

110. ANSWERS

1. Le Havre.
2. Don Profundo.
3. George Antheil.
4. *Candide.*
5. Atlas.
6. *New Year.*
7. Crete.
8. Poland.

9. Italy.
10. The Cape of Good Hope.
11. A sleigh.
12. *Chérubin.*
13. *The Ice Break.*
14. The Mikado.
15. Munich.

Extra Credit:

A. The Prague-Budegovice Express (Second Class).
B. Tony.
C. Sloane Square and South Kensington.

111. ANSWERS

1. Terence McNally.
2. Zoe Caldwell.
3. Twenty-five.
4. *The Lisbon Traviata.*
5. 5/20/58.
6. Claude-Michel Schönberg and Alain Boublil (Richard Maltby, Jr. translated and added lyrics).
7. Jonathan Pryce (it was felt that he was inappropriate casting for a Eurasian).
8. *Old Wicked Songs.*
9. *Rent.*
10. Jonathan Larse.

11. Charles Hart.
12. Ubaldo Piangi.
13. Paris Opéra.
14. David Henry Hwang.
15. Spiro Malas.

Extra Credit:*

"Hannibal" by Chalumeau, "Il Muto" by Albrizzio, and "Don Juan Triumphant" by the Phantom himself.

*Score one point for each correct title or composer.

112. ANSWERS

1. Friedrich de la Motte Fouqué.
2. Huldbrand von Ringstetten (called "Hugo" in the Lortzing work).
3. Seymour Barab (*Ondine*).
4. Dvořák.
5. The three water sprites who open the work.
6. Ježibaba.
7. Dargomijsky.
8. Pushkin.
9. Natasha.
10. Volkhova.
11. The Akian Sea.
12. Catalani's *Elda*, later known as *Loreley*.
13. *Das Rheinnixen*.
14. Rinaldo.
15. Hans Christian Andersen (*Nokken*).

Extra Credit:

A. Mendelssohn.
B. Tchaikovsky's *Undina*.
C. Purcell's *King Arthur*.

113. ANSWERS

1. g
2. f
3. e

4. i
5. h
6. b

7. d
8. j
9. c
10. a
11. m

12. k
13. n
14. o
15. l

Extra Credit:

A. *Give Us This Night.*
B. *Oh…Rosalinda!!*
C. *North Star.*

114. ANSWERS

1. *Der Silbersee.*
2. Ned Rorem.
3. *Gasparone.*
4. *I Masnadieri.*
5. *Les Brigands.*
6. Mrs. Bentson.
7. Samosa.
8. His buddy, the boatswain, loves its landlady and hopes to win her heart by rescuing her.
9. Marquis di San Marco.
10. Raffaelle.
11. Gennaro.
12. Gin.
13. Laetitia.
14. Guillot de Morfontaine.
15. John Adams.

Extra Credit:*

In order: French, English, and German.

*Score two points for each language only if in correct order.

115. ANSWERS

1. *Lady Macbeth of Mtsensk.*
2. Maria Ewing.
3. *Hérodiade.*

4. *Thaïs.*
5. *Rasputin.*
6. Thomas Hampson.
7. *Khovanshchina.*
8. *Sapho.*
9. *Susannah.*
10. After his father's funeral he is royally garbed to receive the double crowns of Upper and Lower Egypt (no pun intended).
11. He is a hermaphrodite. The singer portraying Akhnaten must wear a close-fitting bodysuit molded accordingly.
12. *Isabeau.*
13. Angelica.
14. *Die Soldaten.*
15. Douglas Moore.

Extra Credit:

A. At a tea ceremony in the Nanzenji temple.
B. Several of the ladies-in-waiting went topless.
C. *The Dreyfus Affair.*

116. ANSWERS

1. *Sacco and Vanzetti.*
2. Rimsky-Korsakov.
3. *Moses und Aron.*
4. Gounod.
5. *Le Duc d'Albe.*
6. His pupil, Philipp Jarnach.
7. *Brisëis.*
8. Ben Jonson's *The Devil Is an Ass.*
9. *The Emerald Isle.*
10. *Arizona Lady.*
11. Gerald Tyrwhitt.
12. His wife, Elsa.
13. *Mlada.*
14. *Lo Sposo Deluso.*
15. Leone Emanuele.

Extra Credit:

A. *Rodrigue et Chimène.*
B. César Franck.
C. *The Beggar's Opera.*

117. ANSWERS

1. "The Japanese equivalent for Hear, Hear, Hear!"—literally!
2. China.
3. China.
4. Japan.
5. Nagasaki.
6. 1894 (just for the record, *Madama Butterfly* had its world premiere in 1904).
7. Ceylon
8. Japan.
9. Offenbach.
10. Chabrier.
11. Sidney Jones.
12. Messager.
13. John Adams.
14. Judith Weir.
15. Yup, it's "Made in Japan."

Extra Credit:

A. *The Savage Land.*
B. The director, set designer, and costume designer were all Japanese
C. Eugene Perry.

118. ANSWERS

1. Lady Sangazure *The Sorcerer.*
2. Bunthorne *Patience.*
3. Jane *Patience.*
4. Yum-Yum *The Mikado.*
5. Elizabeth I *Gloriana.*
6. Princess Ida.
7. A jar of rouge.
8. A comb.
9. Baron Ochs.
10. Roucher.
11. A bald head, wig in hand.
12. Pagliacci, in *"Vesti la giubba."*
13. Bella *The Midsummer Marriage.*
14. Harry Easter *Street Scene*
15. Philine *Mignon.*

Extra Credit:*

A. A lady dying her hair "chemical yellow" or "puce," or who "pinches her figger."
B. Lotion to darken his skin, skin toner, and eye makeup.
C. "Paint" for her cheeks, "carmine" for her lips, and face powder.

*Score one point for each correct item (total possible points: nine).

119. ANSWERS

1. Donizetti.
2. Respighi.
3. *"Où va la jeune hindoue?"*
4. Delibes.
5. Planquette.
6. Germaine.
7. The bells will spontaneously ring when the castle's rightful heir arrives.
8. "Any man giving him aid, by word or deed."
9. *Pagliacci.*
10. *Rusalka.*
11. Guillot de Morfontaine.
12. *Le Nozze di Figaro.*
13. Saint-Germain de l'Auxerrois.
14. A tocsin (alarm bell).
15. Cendrillon.

Extra Credit:*

A. *La Grand-Duchesse de Gérolstein.*
B. Something to settle his stomach, throat lozenges, and pills for his wife.
C. Sir Joseph Porter, Josephine, and Captain Corcoran.

*Score two points for A, one point for each item in B and C.

120. ANSWERS

1. An anchor.
2. Ellen.
3. The San Gennaro Festival.
4. *The Last Savage.*

5. Melissa.
6. Lisa *The Grand Duke*.
7. *La Bohème*. (Their laughter is at Musetta.)
8. Elise.
9. Marguerite.
10. *"Il ne revient pas"* (in her oft-cut scene with Siebel).
11. Robin Starveling.
12. *Der Fliegende Holländer*.
13. *Postcard From Morocco*.
14. Brown.
15. "Adam and Eve's Expulsion From the Garden."

Extra Credit:

A. *"Tela"* (embroidery canvas) and silk.
B. Lilies and roses.
C. *The Mother of Us All*.

121. ANSWERS*

A.	7	c		I.	11	a
B.	6	f		J.	8	n
C.	1	j		K.	7	m
D.	2	h		L.	4	g
E.	10	b		M.	12	k
F.	3	e		N.	5	d
G.	1	l		O.	9	i
H.	11	o				

*Score one point per correct item (total possible points: thirty).

122. ANSWERS*

A.	14	g		I.	4	j
B.	5	b		J.	11	d
C.	7	m		K.	12	e
D.	13	f		L.	2	o
E.	9	c		M.	10	l
F.	6	n		N.	2	h
G.	8	a		O.	1	k
H.	3	i				

*Score one point for each correct match (total possible points: thirty).

123. ANSWERS

1. Angela Gheorghiu.
2. The Cherry Duet from *L'Amico Fritz* (they were married 4/26/96 by Mayor Giuliani. See Extra Credit question C for more about him).
3. Licia Albanese, who was outraged by its eroticism.
4. Renée Fleming.
5. The Countess Almaviva, of course.
6. Bryn Terfel.
7. The Shepherd Boy in *Tosca*.
8. Jennifer Larmore.
9. Telramund, with San Francisco Opera.
10. Barbara Hendricks.
11. Plácido Domingo.
12. Ara Beberian, who sang Benoit at the Met and then Alcindoro at the Detroit Opera House.
13. William Parker.
14. Harolyn Blackwell.
15. Gegam Grigorian.

Extra Credit:*

A. The Baths of Caracalla, in Rome, on the eve of the World Cup soccer finals (it was such an extraordinary event that the Rome airport even rerouted its flights away from the vicinity!).
B. Montserrat Caballé, Teresa Berganza, Giacomo Aragall, José Carreras, Plácido Domingo, and Juan Pons, who lip-synched their previously recorded material.
C. "*O Sole Mio.*"

*Score one point per item in A and B, two points for C.

124. ANSWERS

1. Siegfried.
2. *Le Comte Ory.*
3. Godvino.
4. Roland.
5. Hidraot, King of Damascus.
6. *Les Abencérages.*
7. Rutland Boughton.
8. Fernand *La Favorite.*
9. John Tomlinson.
10. *La Tribute de Zamora.*
11. *Don Rodrigo.*
12. Oronte.
13. *Zaira.*
14. *I Capuleti e i Montecchi.*
15. *Dom Sébastien.*

Extra Credit:*

A. *Zoraide di Granata* and *Alahor in Granata*.
B. Goffredo, Rinaldo, Gernando, Carlo, Eustazio, and Ubaldo.
C. Though the role had indeed been composed for Giovanni Battista Velluti, "last of the great male sopranos," who had also performed it at *Crociato's* world premiere in Venice, a castrato had not been heard on the London stage for twenty-five years. (Once they got over their initial astonishment, he did become a hit with the Brits.)

*Score one point for each name or title in A and B, two points for C.

125. ANSWERS

1. *Treemonisha.*
2. Crown, in *Porgy and Bess.*
3. Mistletoe.
4. *Rinaldo.*
5. Nika Magadoff.
6. A giant oak tree.
7. By holding on to Mefistofele's cloak.
8. In tea.
9. 70 St. Mary Axe.
10. Taven.
11. Ortrud.
12. A dragon.
13. Lamère Grabille.
14. Le Marquis de Saluces.
15. Alfred Cellier.

Extra Credit:*

A. The Queen of Hearts, the Two of Spades, and the Queen of Hearts again.
B. Ormus.
C. Kashesh.

*Score one point for each of the three draws in A, two points per B and C.

126. ANSWERS

1. Jennifer Larmore.
2. Jane Eaglen.
3. Montserrat Martí.
4. Freddie Mercury.
5. Jochen Kowalski.
6. Sally Burgess.
7. Josephine Barstow.
8. *Le Domino Noir.*
9. *Aida.*
10. Joan Sutherland.
11. Leontyne Price.
12. *Les Troyens.*
13. "Songs of the Cat."
14. Sumi Jo.
15 Richard Conrad.

Extra Credit:*

A. Wilhelmenia Fernandez/Sharon Benson (Carmen) and Damon Evans/Michael Austin (Joe).

B. Meriel Dickinson (Emma Jones), Blythe Duff (Shirley Kaplan), and Matthew Costello (Vincent Jones).

C. In 1994, before he became director of the Scottish Opera, John Mauceri conducted the New York City Opera *Candide*. The Scottish Opera *Candide* was recorded in 1988 under his administration, but conducted by Justin Brown!

*Score one point for each singer in A, for each singer or role in B, for each conductor in C.

127. ANSWERS

1. Italian.
2. Mattia Battistini.
3. Corno di Bassetto.
4. F-sharp, one of the highest notes asked of a soprano in opera.
5. *Alessandro Stradella.*
6. *Bianca und Giuseppe.*
7. Manuella Hoelterhoff, opera critic of the *Wall Street Journal.*
8. Benjamin Franklin.
9. Michael Balfe.
10. Excellenz Silva.
11. *Gustave III ou Le Bal Masqué*, composed by Auber. Verdi's *Un Ballo in Maschera,* based on this opera, employs a different libretto.
12. *Ivanhoe.*
13. Victor Herbert (he played the cello).
14. *Carmen.*
15. Janáček's *Osud*

Extra Credit:

A. His high D.
B. D.
C. C.

128. ANSWERS

1. *Owen Wingrave*.
2. Swan Vestas.
3. *"Celui que j'exercise"* ("The same as mine").
4. *Conchita*.
5. *The King Goes Forth to France*.
6. *"Matrimonio Presto,"* whose *M* and *P* she claims she reads in Dorabella's palm.
7. He has a spatula mark on his right arm.
9. *Il Viaggio a Reims*.
10. Vassar.
11. Mardian.
12. *La Princesse Jaune*.
13. *Cox and Box*.
14. *Deseret* (composed by Leonard Kastle).
15. Capricorn.

Extra Credit:

A. Regalias, Auroras, and Eurekas.
B. *L'Amico Fritz* and *Le Juif Polonais,* respectively.
C. Edwin and Angelina (could Gilbert have been thinking of the second-ever U.S. opera, *Edwin and Angelina*, performed only once in 1796? Nah...).

129. ANSWERS

1. Jane Eaglen.
2. Carol Vaness.
3. Stuart Neill (his second, and last, encore was "The Lord's Prayer"—unaccented).
4. Richard Tauber.
5. François Le Roux.
6. He became one of the few tenors in history to sing both Siegfried and Siegmund in the same *Ring* cycle.
7. Joan Sutherland.
8. Jessye Norman.
9. Theodore Wachtel.
10. Helga Dernesch.
11. Frank Lopardo.

12. Dawn Upshaw.
13. Martin Thompson.
14. Ivan Kozlovsky, who, though he did not sing at the event, played the piano.
15. MEFISTO.

Extra Credit:*

A. Eugene and Herbert Perry.
B. Mirella Freni and Luciano Pavarotti, in 1935.
C. Esther (Norma), Ruby (Adalgisa), and Grace (Clotilda) Hinds.

*Score one point per correct singer.

130. ANSWERS

1. He felt it was pirated from his own "Home, Sweet Home," and that Donizetti had violated copyright laws.
2. His first, *Almira*.
3. Gustave Doré.
4. Jerome Hines.
5. *La Cenerentola*.
6. *Der Cid* (based on the play that also inspired Massenet's *Le Cid*).
7. Seattle Opera.
8. Ferdinando Paer; the opera was *Camilla*.
9. *Stiffelio*.
10. *Die Schweigsame Frau*.
11. *Roberto Devereux*. "God Save the King/Queen," used in the overture, had not yet been composed in Queen Elizabeth's day.
12. Salvatore Cammarano.
13. *El Retablo de Maese Pedro* ("Master Peter's Puppet Show").
14. *Nerone*.
15. *Faust*.

Extra Credit:*

A. A secondary personality of William Sharp, who had such a complete psychological break from his alter ego that they corresponded with each other in writing to communicate.
B. The composer, Erich Korngold, and his father, Julius Korngold.
C. *Vanessa, La Traviata,* and *Turandot*.

*Score four points for A, and two points for each correct item in B and C

Appendix

WORKS FEATURED IN THIS BOOK

Below, a list of all operas, operettas, and musical comedies contained in *What's Your Opera I.Q.?* Plays and movies based upon, or featuring performance or performers of. classical vocal material, are also included.

For reader accessibility, works better known to the West by their English or (as occurs with several Russian operas) French titles are listed as such throughout the book; Items followed by a number are identically titled works by more than one composer.

The Abduction of Figaro
Les Abencérages
Acis and Galatea
Adrianna Lecouvreur
L'Africaine
Die Agyptische Helena
Aida
L'Aiglon
Akhnaten
Alahor in Granata
Albert Herring
Alceste
Aleko
Alessandro
Alessandro Stradella
L'Almira
Amadeus

Amahl and the Night Visitors
Amelia Goes to the Ball
L'Amico Fritz
El Amor Brujo
Amore del Tre Re
L'Amore Medico
L'Amour Masqué
And the Ship Sails On (film)
Andrea Chénier
Angélique
Aniara
Anna Bolena
Antony and Cleopatra
Anush
Apocalypse Now (film)
Arabella
Aria (film)

Ariadne auf Naxos
Ariodante
Arizona Lady
Arlecchino
L'Arlesiana
Armida
Armide
Aroldo
Arrianna
  Abbandonada
Artaserse
The Aspern Papers (2)
At the Boar's Head
Atlántida
Atlas
Attila
Atys
Aureliano in Palmira
Azora

Baa Baa Black Sheep
Babar the Elephant
The Ballad of Baby Doe
Un Ballo in Maschera
Il Barbiere di Siviglia (2)
Barkouf
The Bartered Bride
Bastien und Bastienne
Ba-ta-clan
La Battaglia di Legnano
The Bear
Beatrice di Tenda
Béatrice et Bénédict
Beatrix Cenci
Because You're Mine (film)
Before Breakfast
The Beggar's Opera

La Belle et le Bête
La Belle Hélène
Betrothal in a Monastery
Bianca und Giuseppe
The Big Broadcast of 1938 (film)
Billy Budd
The Blond Eckbert
Blue Monday
The Boatswain's Mate
La Bohème (2)
The Bohemian Girl
Bolivar
Les Boréades
Boris Godunov
Boulevard Solitude
The Bride From Pluto
Brigadoon
Les Brigands
Briséïs

Cabildo
Cadmus et Hermione
Call Me Mister (album)
La Cambiale di Matrimonio
Camilla
La Campana Sommersa
Il Campanello di Notte
Candide
Il Cappello di Paglia di Firenze
Capriccio
Captain Jinks of the Horse
  Marines
I Capuletti e i Montecchi
Cardillac
Carmen
Carmen (film)
Carmen Jones (film)

Carmina Burana
Carousel
Casanova
Cats
Cavalleria Rusticana
Cendrillon
La Cenerentola
Chérubin
Le Cheval de Bronze
Christóbal Colón
Christophe Colomb
Christopher Columbus
Der Cid
Le Cid
Cinderella
La Clamenza di Tito
Cleofide
Les Cloches de Corneville
Colas et Colinette
Le Comte Ory
Conchita
The Consul
Les Contes d'Hoffmann
Le Convenienze Teatrali
Le Coq d'Or
Il Corsaro
Una Cosa Rara
Così Fan Tutte
Cox and Box
The Cradle Will Rock
La Créole
The Cricket on the Hearth
Crispino e la Comare
Cristoforo Colombo
Il Crociato in Egitto
The Crucible

Die Csárdásfürstin
The Cunning Little Vixen

Dalibor
La Dame Blanche
La Damnation de Faust
The Dangerous Liaisons
Daphne
Death in Venice
The Death of Klinghoffer
Deidamia
Deseret
Les Deux Aveugles
The Devil and Daniel Webster
The Devil and Kate
The Devils of Loudon
The Devil's Wall
Le Devin du Village
Dialogues des Carmélites
Diana von Solange
Dido and Aeneas
Dinorah
Distant Harmony (film)
Diva (film)
Divas (film)
Le Docteur Miracle (2)
Le Docteur Ox
Doctor Faustus Lights the Lights
Doktor Faust
Die Dollarprinzessin
Dom Sébastien
Le Domino Noir
Don Carlos
Don Giovanni
Don Pasquale
Don Procopio

Don Quichotte
Don Rodrigo
Don Sanche
La Donna del Lago
Le Donne Curiose
The Dream of Valentino
Dreamkeepers
Die Drei Pintos
Drei Wälzer
The Dreyfus Affair
Le Duc d'Albe
Il Due Foscari
Duke Bluebeard's Castle

L'Eclair
Edgar
Edwin and Angelina
Einstein on the Beach
Elegy for Young Lovers
Elektra
Elisabetta, Regina d'Inghilterra
L'Elisir d'Amore
The Emerald Isle
Emmeline
The Emperor Jones
The Emperor's New Clothes
L'Enfant et les Sortilèges
Die Englische Katz
Die Entführung aus dem Serail
Ercole Amante
Ernani
Erwartung
Esclarmonde
Esther
L'Etoile
L'Etoile du Nord

Eugene Onegin
Euryanthe
The Excursions of Mr. Brouček

The Fairy Queen
Falstaff
La Fanciulla del West
Farewell My Concubine (film)
Farinelli (film)
Faust
La Favola d'Orfeo
La Favorite
Fedora
Die Feen
Fernando Cortez
Fidelio
Fierrabras
The Fiery Angel
La Fille de Madame Angot
La Fille du Régiment
La Fille du Tambour-Major
La Finta Giardiniera
La Finta Semplice
Fisch-Ton-Can
Fitzcarraldo (film)
Die Fledermaus
Der Fliegende Holländer
Follies
La Forza del Destino
Foul Play (film)
Four Saints in Three Acts
Fra Diavolo
Fra i Due Litiganti
Francesca da Rimini
Frau Luna
Die Frau ohne Schatten

Der Freischütz
The Frogs
From the House of the Dead
Il Furioso nell'Isola di San
  Domingo

Gallantry
The Gambler
Gasparone
El Gato Montés
Gawain
La Gazza Ladra
La Gazzetta
Die Geburtstag der Infantin
The Geisha
Genoveva
Germania
Ghisèle
The Ghosts of Versailles
Gianni Schicchi
Giants of the Earth
La Gioconda
I Gioielli della Madonna
Un Giorno di Regno
Giulio Cesare
Give Us This Night (film)
Gloriana
The Gondoliers
Die Götterdämmerung
The Good Soldier Schweik
Goya
The Grand Duke
La Grande-Duchesse de
  Gérolstein
The Great Victor Herbert (film)
The Great Waltz (film)

Grisélidis
Il Guarany
Guest of Honor
Guglielmo Ratcliff
Guillaume Tell
Guntram
Gustave III ou Le Bal Masqué

Halka
A Hand of Bridge
Hänsel und Gretel
Harriet: The Woman Called
  Moses
Harvey Milk
Háry János
Help, Help, the Globolinks!
Henry VIII
Hérodiade
L'Heure Espagnole
L'Histoire de Babar
Higglety Pigglety Pop!
Hin und Zurück
Hippolyte et Aricie
H.M.S. Pinafore
Hugh the Drover
Les Huguenots
Hunyady László
Le Huron

I Am the Way
The Ice Break
Idomeneo
I Dream Too Much (film)
L'Ile de Rêve
The Immortal Hour
Immortal Beloved (film)

L'Incoronazione di Poppea
Les Indes Galantes
The Indian Queen
The Insect Comedy
Intermezzo
In the Shadow of the Stars (film)
Iolanthe
Iphigénie en Tauride
Iris
Isabeau
The Island God
L'Italiana in Algeri
It's a Date (film)
Ivan IV
Ivanhoe

Jeanne d'Arc au Bûcher
Jenůfa
Jesus
The Jewel Box
La Jolie Fille de Perth
Le Jongleur de Notre-Dame
Le Juif Polonais
La Juive
Julien
Julietta
The Jumping Frog of Calaveras
    County
Der Junge Lord
The Juniper Tree

Kát'ya Kabanová
Khovanshchina
King Arthur
The King Goes Forth to France
King Priam

King Roger
Kinkakuji
Kismet
Kiss Me Kate
Königskinder

Lady Macbeth of Mtsensk
Lakmé
Das Land die Lachëlns
The Last Savage
Leonora
The Libertine
Libuše
Die Liebe der Danae
Das Liebesverbot
A Life for the Tsar
Life With an Idiot
Linda di Chamounix
The Lisbon Traviata
A Little Night Music
The Little Sweep
Lizzie Borden
La Loca
Lodoletta
Lohengrin
I Lombardi
Lord Byron
Loreley (2)
Lost in the Stars
Lou Salomé
Louise
The Love for Three Oranges
Lucia di Lammermoor
Lucrezia
Lucrezia Borgia
Luisa Miller
Lulu

Die Lustige Witwe

Die Lustigen Weiber von Windsor

M. Butterfly

Macbeth

Madama Butterfly

Madame Adare

Madame l'Archiduc

Madame Butterfly (film)

Madame Chrysanthème

Madame Favart

Madame Pompadour

Madame Sans-Gêne

The Making of the Representative for Planet 8

The Makropoulos Affair

Les Malheurs d'Orphée

Les Mamelles de Tirésias

Mam-zelle Fifi

Mam-zelle Nitouche

The Man Who Mistook His Wife for a Hat

Manon

Manon Lescaut (2)

Manru

Maometto II

Maria di Rohan

Maria di Rudenz

Maria Golovin

Maria Stuarda

Marilyn

Marino Faliero

Martha

Mary, Queen of Scots

Maskarade

I Masnadieri

Master Class

Mathis der Maler

Matilde di Shabran

Il Matrimonio Segreto

Mavra

Maximilien

McTeague

Le Médecin Malgré Lui

Médée (2)

The Medium

Meeting Venus (film)

Mefistofele

Die Meistersinger

Merrily We Roll Along

Merry Mount

Mesdames de la Halle

Metropolitan (film)

The Midnight Angel

The Midsummer Marriage

A Midsummer Night's Dream

The Mighty Casey

Mignon

The Mikado

Mimi (film)

Minutes Till Midnight

Mireille

Miss Havisham's Fire

Miss Julie

Miss Saigon

Mitridate Eupatore

Mitridate, Rè di Ponto

Mlada

Mlle. Modiste

Modern Painters

Les Mohicans

Moïse et Pharaon

Der Mond
Il Mondo della Luna
Monsieur Beaucaire
Monsieur Choufleuri
Montezuma
Moonstruck (film)
Mosè in Egitto
Moses und Aron
The Most Happy Fella
The Most Important Man
The Mother of Three Sons
The Mother of Us All
The Mountebanks
Mozart and Salieri
The Mozart Brothers (film)
Mrs. Dalloway
La Muette de Portici
The Music Man
The Music Teacher (film)
My Fair Lady
My Heart's in the Highlands

Nabucco
Natoma
Naughty Marietta
Nerone
New Year
A Night at the Chinese Opera
Nine Rivers from Jordan
Nixon in China
Noë
Nokken
Norma
North Star (film)
The Nose
Noyes Fludde
Le Nozze di Figaro

L'Oca del Cairo
L'Occasione Fa il Ladro
Oedipus Rex
Of Mice and Men
Oh...Rosalinda!! (film)
L'Oiseau Bleu
The Old Maid and the Thief
Old Wicked Songs (play)
Ondine
100 Men and a Girl (film)
1000 Airplanes on the Roof
Orfeo ed Euridice
Orlando
Ormindo
Orphée aux Enfers
Orphée et Eurydice
Osud
Otello
Otello (film)
Otto Mesi in Due Oro
Owen Wingrave

Pacific Overtures
Padmâvati
Pagliacci
The Pajama Game
Palestrina
The Pardoner's Tale
Parisina
Parsifal
Passion
The Passion of Jonathan Wade
Patience
Patience and Sarah
Paul Bunyan
Les Pêcheurs de Perles
Pelléas et Mélisande

Pénélope
La Périchole
La Perle du Brésil
Peter Grimes
Peter Ibbetson
The Phantom of the Opera
Philémon et Baucis
Phoebus and Pan
La Pietra del Paragone
The Pilgrim's Progress
Il Pirata
The Pirates of Penzance
La Pomme d'Api
Porgy and Bess
Postcard from Morocco
Le Postillon de Longjumeau
The Postman Always Rings Twice
Pousse d'Amour
Le Pré aux Clercs
Pretty Woman (film)
Prima la Musica e poi le Parole
Prince Igor
Princess Ida
La Princess Jaune
Der Protagonist
I Puritani
Puss in Boots

I Quattro Rusteghi
The Queen of Spades
A Question of Taste
A Quiet Place

The Rake's Progress
The Rape of Lucretia
Rasputin
Regina

Il Re Pastore
La Reine de Saba
Rent
El Retablo de Maese Pédro
Das Rheingold
Das Rheinnixen
Riders to the Sea
Rienzi
Rigoletto
Rinaldo
The Ring Cycle
    Das Rheingold
    Die Walküre
    Siegfried
    Götterdämmerung
Rip Van Winkle
The Robbers
Robert le Diable
Roberto Devereux
Rodrigo
Rodrigue et Chimène
Le Roi de Lahore
Le Roi d'Ys
Le Roi L'A Dit
Le Roi Malgré Lui
Roman River
Roméo et Juliette
La Rondine
Der Rosenkavalier
Le Rossignol
Ruddigore
Rusalka

Sacco and Vanzetti
Sadko
Saint Elisabeth
The Saint of Bleeker Street

Salome
Samson
Samson et Dalila
San Francisco (film)
Sapho (2)
The Saracen
Satyagraha
The Savage Land
Die Schatzkammer des Inka
Die Schauspieldirektor
Lo Schiavo
Die Schweigsame Frau
The Second Hurricane
Semele
Semiramide
Serse
La Serva Padrona
The Seven Deadly Sins
Show Boat
Le Siège de Corinth
The Siege of Rhodes
Siegfried
Il Signor Bruschino
Der Silbersee
Simon Boccanegra
Simón Bolívar
Sir John in Love
Six Characters in Search of an
   Author
Die Soldaten
Song O' My Heart (film)
Song of Norway
La Sonnambula
The Sorcerer
The Sound of Music
Sous le Masque

South Pacific
Lo Sposo Deluso
Stiffelio
The Stone Guest
The Story of a Real Man
Street Scene
The Student From Salamanca
Summer and Smoke
Suor Angelica
Susannah
Sweeney Todd

Il Tabarro
Tales of Hoffman (film)
Tamerlano
Tancredi
Tannhäuser
Der Tapfere Soldat
Tausendundeine Nacht
Taverner
The Temple of Minerva
The Tender Land
Thaïs
Thespis
The Threepenny Opera
Tiefland
Titon et l'Aurore
Tobermory
Tosca
Die Tote Stadt
La Tragédie de Carmen
Transatlantic
Transformations
La Traviata
La Traviata (film)
Treemonisha

Trial by Jury
La Tribute de Zamora
Tristan und Isolde
Troilus and Cressida
Trouble in Tahiti
Troubled Island
Il Trovatore
Les Troyens
The Tsar's Bride
Turandot
Il Turco in Italia
The Turn of the Screw
The Two Widows

Undina
Undine (2)
Utopia Limited

Vanessa
Les Vêpres Siciliennes
La Vera Storia
Das Verratene Meer
Die Versunkene Cloche
La Vestale
Il Viaggio a Reims
La Vie Parisienne
Le Villi
Viola
The Voice of Ariadne
La Voix Humaine
The Voyage
La Voyage dans la Lune

Wagner (film)
Die Walküre
La Wally
Ein Walzertraum
War and Peace
Werther
West Side Story
Where the Wild Things Are
The White Horse Inn
Der Wildschütz
The Wings of a Dove
The Witches of Eastwick (film)
The Wreckers
Wozzeck
A Wrinkle in Time
Wuthering Heights (2)

X

The Yellow Wallpaper
The Yeomen of the Guard
Yes, Giorgio (film)
Yolanta

Zaïda
Zaira
Zar und Zimmerman
Die Zauberflöte
Zazà
Der Zigeunerbaron
The Zoo
Zoraide di Granata
Zwei Herzen im Dreivierteltakt

About the Author

Iris Bass grew up listening to the Texaco Opera Quiz and its surrounding Metropolitan Opera matinee broadcasts, in that order of interest. One of her earliest opera-related memories is of laughing herself silly over Milton Cross's description of Gilda's murder. Since falling utterly in love with live performance while in her late teens—the turning point was a New York City Opera *Le Coq d'Or*—she has attended hundreds of opera performances in the United States and abroad. She still thinks that business with the sack leaves something to be desired.

For ten years, Iris served as editor of *Sightlines*, an opera journal published by Opera Glass, an audience organization she cofounded in 1984. She works in the editorial department of a major publishing house and, an affiliate member of Opera America, is also a freelance consultant specializing in opera-performer résumés.

Her eclectic musical tastes have a particular slant toward French opera, Rossini, and stratospheric voices. Iris shares her book- and recording-filled Brooklyn brownstone apartment with four cats: Sophie, Baby Doe, Jenůfa, and Regina, who have collectively dismantled a stereo speaker to look for the voices.